Starc

The Inc

Stardust Ranch: The Incredible True Story

Copyright 2019-2020 ©John Edmonds and Bruce MacDonald. All rights reserved. Hardcover book

ISBN: 978-09921328-7-3

Published by BCI, Toronto, Ontario, Canada

for my wife Joyce

The world is a fine place and worth fighting for...

— Ernest Hemingway

Contents

Part I

Introduction

I first met John Edmonds in 2012. A mutual friend contacted me and asked me if I was interested in taking a look at a non-fiction book project. He began to describe a UFO story taking place in Arizona. I was never that interested in the whole world of exopolitics and extraterrestrials. I knew it existed. I didn't disbelieve it. It just wasn't on my radar. At that time, the only book I had published to good reviews was a work of adult literary fiction in Canada. I fancied myself a kind of Canadian Mark Twain, a humorist and social observer. I got very good reviews across Canada, but my second novel didn't publish. My living comes from technical writing in telecommunications and software.

After persistent badgering from my friend, I decided to have a chat with John Edmonds. The three of us got together on a conference call and John began to tell me what was going on at his ranch. I wouldn't say that I was skeptical, it's just that I really wasn't that interested. I had read the Billy Meier work about the Pleiadian contact in Switzerland, and I found all of that to be a bit dubious. My fundamental question was what impact does this have on humanity? Why should people be giving their time to this topic? How is it any more important than us becoming a more cooperative and compassionate species so that we can survive on this planet? After some persuasion, I decided to give the book a try. John Edmonds and I set up a working process. We talked on Skype every day and I recorded the conversations and started to write. After some months of this I quit. I can't really describe what happened back then. I became very negative towards the material. It was the only manuscript I never finished.

Seven years went by and I never gave the book on Stardust Ranch a second thought. My life changed dramatically. I decided to leave North America and go into the wilds of Costa Rica. I bought some land in the rainforest in the south of Costa Rica, a place known as the Talamanca mountain range, designated a United Nations Educational Scientific and Cultural Organization (UNESCO) heritage site. It might well be the most biodiverse thousand square kilometers in the world.

I brought my eighteen-year-old son over when he finished high school. He wasn't sure what he wanted to do, and he wanted to take some time off before he went to post-secondary education or into a trade. So father and son made their way into the rainforest and began to build earthbag houses. It was a wonderful project and we both learned Spanish and grew into the little *campesino* culture on the mountain, which is a mix of Ticos and Cabecare natives. Jaguars roam the mountains. Howler monkeys scream through the jungle at dawn with a mating call that is the loudest sound in nature, the decibel level exceeding a rock concert. When walking off-road, knee-high boots are mandatory because of the many varieties of snakes, more than a few of them being venomous. The insect world is equally fascinating — spiders that can kill a horse with an ankle bite, praying mantises of exquisite composition and beauty, bullet ants, named so because their bite is more painful than being shot, and too many other insects to name and describe. The birds are glorious, wild parrots and hummingbirds of magnificent color and beauty. The Talamanca mountains are a magical place. I've lived here for three years now, continuing with my trade of technical writing through remote work. I liberated myself from Toronto, Canada, learned to grow food and raise animals, and now I have fifty banana plants, pineapple, a large garden, a pig pen, a chicken coop, and I'm thinking of raising rabbits. I buy milk and cheese from a Nicaraguan neighbor with a cow. In summation, I utterly unplugged myself from my middle class upbringing in Ottawa and my twenty year career in technology in Toronto. I own my time. This is a very beautiful feeling I wish on everybody. Time is the real currency in a human life — time to read the classic books and sacred poetry, time to meditate in a sacramental way, time to walk my dog through the dirt roads and paths crisscrossing the mountains, and time to do the work I want to do. Then something truly odd started. I began getting visits from UFOs. My neighbors took pictures of large orbs over my house and showed them to me. Something started happening inside the house. There was a weird smell, something like copper, rubbing alcohol, and blood mixed together. I had the distinct impression that something was visiting me. It was around this time that I started to think back to the failed book project with John Edmonds. I had also been reminded of John at the end of 2017 when his story went national in the press. Everybody was talking about it, most of the print media outlets and a lot of the broadcasters. I reached out to him and we spoke briefly. It was decided that we would start the book again and this time we would finish it.

I'll give you an overview of the story with the *New York Post*.

Man desperately trying to sell his 'alien-infested'ranch

By Gabrielle Fonrouge October 26, 2017 | 1:58pm | Updated

An Arizona man has put his ranch up for sale — because he says he's been harassed for years by aliens who even tried to abduct his wife, reports said.

John Edmonds, owner of the Stardust Ranch in Rainbow Valley, about an hour west of Phoenix, is a popular figure in the alien believers community and has publicized his purported encounters with extraterrestrials on Facebook, claiming it's the reason he wants to sell his ranch, 12News TV reported.

"They actually levitated my wife out of the bed in the master chamber and carried her into the parking lot and tried to draw her up into the craft," he said, according to the outlet.

"This is why I want to move!"

He said that in the past 20 years, he has experienced many "strange events" involving aliens and claims to have killed more than a dozen extraterrestrials on his sprawling ranch.

A photo posted to his Facebook in March shows a bloodied samurai sword in a pool of what looks like dried blood from an alien he says he killed March 13. In another photo, he shows a picture of a wound on his calf and wrote that it came from an alien.

"Wounds from recent attack here at Stardust Ranch upper right calf from battle with malevolent ET," he wrote.

The property has been featured on "Ghost Adventures" on the Travel Channel and has garnered international attention. He recommends anyone interested in the $5 million property be "very well-grounded.

"It's not something for a traditional family, but it holds a lot of secrets and what I believe are future opportunities to understand forces that are in the universe.

"Please be very well-grounded because the energy here has the tendency to manifest with whatever is going on with you," he said.

I can assure you that John's whole story has never been told. There are aspects of it that he can't quite articulate to the headline seeking media, or to television programs interested only in the paranormal. This is the whole story of Stardust Ranch.

— Bruce MacDonald

Part II

The First Few Years

Chapter 1

An Ominous Foreshadowing

I was born in the late nineteen-fifties and grew up in a bad neighbor-hood in Evanston, Illinois. I had to learn to be aware of my surround-ings at all times. There was a danger in violence all around me. The only rest I had from this was visiting my grandfather in rural Arkansas. He was a Cherokee Indian. He lived on a small farm in the woods. Somehow this dichotomy of the tough Evanston neighborhood and my grandfather's farm in the woods instilled in me a great dream of one day living in nature. I grew up and I went to school and I became a psychiatric counselor. In my early thirties, I moved to Arizona, opened up a practice there, and met my wife Joyce.

In the mid-nineties, I became tired of the hustle and bustle of life in Phoenix, Arizona. I wanted to realize my dream of owning a ranch and having horses and space that I could call my own with neighbors too far away to even hear. My wife Joyce and I contacted a Realtor in Arizona and told him what we were looking for, which was a decent-sized ranch of at least ten acres that had a large living quarter on it and the capability to build more. Our budget was limited and therefore the more expensive ranch areas of Arizona were off-limits to us. That left some of the more remote and undeveloped areas that had ranches in Arizona, places like Rainbow Valley, which was undeveloped and re-mote in 1996, an unincorporated municipality outside of Buckeye, nes-tled inside Maricopa County, probably made most famous by Sheriff

Joe Arpaio, who branded himself a no-nonsense southern sheriff in the nineties and early part of the new century, often making headline news for some of his positions on immigration and crime in general. Joe was a storied man, a former head of the Drug Enforcement Agency (DEA) turned small-time sheriff. Phoenix was about forty-five to fifty minutes away, more if the traffic was heavy in the morning or at the end of the workday. Despite the commute, many people lived in Buckeye and worked in Phoenix.

Buckeye was incorporated in the late 1800s and started with a very minuscule population. It now rests at about eighty-five to ninety thousand people. If you look up Stardust Ranch on Google Maps you'll see that it sits within the municipality of Buckeye. In the mid-to-late nineties, Rainbow valley was an affordable part of Arizona — not many people who made their living in Phoenix wanted to drive that far out every morning and back in the evening. Phoenix isn't like other large metropolitan areas that have commuter trains. It's not Evanston or New York. The southwest is just not like that. You have to get in your car and you have to drive everywhere you want to go in the southwest.

After realizing my geographical limitations based on budget, I was amenable to the Realtor showing me ranches for sale in Buckeye, and that led me to Stardust Ranch. Of course, it wasn't named Stardust Ranch in the late nineties. That's a name that it's taken on as its infamy has grown, a name coined by myself and now known around the world.

If you look at Stardust Ranch in the satellite view of Google Maps, you'll see dry hard land with very little green, a kind of orange, red, and brown. It's the kind of land that you'd see in an old west movie, and when you have your feet on the ground in Buckeye, that's exactly what it feels like.

Except for the house itself, which is fairly modern, my ranch looks like it's from an old west movie. It's the kind of hard scab land that a man looking for true solitude would feel comfortable in, and when I saw it I saw my dream.

It was everything I was looking for and more. The main house had about three and a half thousand square feet; it was palatial, a real ranch that could have visitors, horseback riding lessons, an animal shelter, anything I had dreamed. There were five bedrooms and three bathrooms, a large storage room, a huge living room, and a great kitchen that Joyce loved. The construction was fairly new, no more than fifteen or twenty years, and everything was in great condition, including the in-ground pool in the back. It seemed too good to be true. The price was extremely low for the amount of space we were getting, both the house itself and the ten acres that attended it, all fenced off and ready for horse training. There was also a large stable in the back that could easily accommodate twenty horses. The whole time the Realtor was showing me the property I kept thinking, what's the catch? He described it as the deal of a lifetime. The funny thing about wanting something really badly and then having it put right in front of you is all your discernment goes away. You don't ask intelligent questions.

My wife Joyce, who I had only been married to for a few years at the time, was not as taken with the place as I was. Right from the first visit, she had a bad feeling about the place. I was blinded by my desire. My intuition had been muted by my excitement. There were more than a few long conversations at our home in Glendale before we agreed to buy the ranch. I don't know why Joyce was so averse to the place. I do now. I didn't then. She was just expressing her intuition. She had a very bad feeling about the place right from our first visit. It created a little tension in our fairly young marriage. Part of me thought that she was trying to quash my dream. She was not the country bumpkin I was. She didn't want to continue to work in Phoenix with the long commute from the ranch. I thought she was being selfish. She thought I was being selfish. Neither of us knew back then that it had nothing to do with selfishness or whose dream about how we would live would win out. Joyce's intuition was dead on. It always has been. I was too young and too stupid to attend to that intuition back then.

Part of the dream of the ranch for me was a new revenue stream. I had a million and one business ideas for the place. I was already in my mid-to-late thirties a bit burned out from my social work practice. I wouldn't call it a midlife crisis. I was thirty-seven years old when we took the place. It was enough time for me to grow sour on counseling. I didn't want to live my life listening to other people's problems all the time. I enjoyed helping people, there's no doubt about that. If you have ever worked in the therapy fields, psychology, counseling, psychiatry, it's extremely toxic. It takes a part of you away. I really enjoyed what I had done with my skills as a counselor. I was very proud of the people I had helped in my life, but it's not how I saw my life continuing. I was more of a hands-on kind of guy. I wanted to feed horses. I wanted a large dog kennel with nothing but Rottweilers. I wanted nature, and I wanted freedom.

When we saw the ranch it was fully occupied. We didn't meet any people, but it was fully furnished. The Realtor told us that the family used it as a vacation property but didn't live there full-time. I mean it was really decked out. There was beautiful leather furniture in the living room. There were rugs to-die-for. The walls were adorned with art, albeit unoriginal art, most of the stuff was prints, but it was nicely framed and tastefully laid out. The kitchen was completely stocked. There were blenders and mixers and toasters and toaster ovens and a beautiful oven and microwaves and a gorgeous eating table, a solid wood dining room table with eight chairs. The bathroom closets were fully stocked with nearly new towels, hand cloths, a six-month supply of hand soap and shower gel and hair shampoo. Every room was finished. The bedroom sets were really elaborate. There was expensive outdoor furniture around the in-ground pool. The place showed really well. It was a massive moving job for whoever was selling the place. It seemed like a lot of money and one had to wonder where they were going to put all the stuff if this was just a second house they vacationed in, as the Realtor had told us.

In the end, it was the price that made it the selection to fulfill my dream to live on a ranch. I believed my capable hands could turn it into anything I wanted it to be. I was just happy for the land and for the opportunity to live in solitude and to get away from the city of Phoenix. The deal was inked, the contract signed, and cash was paid. I put my entire life savings into the place. Joyce and I were given the keys. I began all of the tasks related to moving into the house.

Pool Contents

About a month later, Joyce and I packed up and loaded all of the contents of our old home into the rental truck and drove out to the new ranch. We had been given the keys just a few days earlier. I still remember that day driving down Tuthill Road in the rented U-Haul truck packed with all of my contents. I had this incredible lightness in me. I felt like a kid on Christmas morning. I can still remember clearly the first time I unlocked the front gate with the U-Haul truck idling behind me. I undid the chain and pushed the two gates open. I looked back at Joyce who was driving behind the truck in our car. I had a big smile on my face. She smiled back. I think she was just infected with my happiness. She had reconciled herself to living at the ranch, but she was not entirely comfortable with it. I drove the U-Haul truck down the long dirt laneway, my eyes glued to the large house. I was beaming with pride.

When we opened the door and walked into the house, we were startled to realize that none of the contents of the house had been removed. My first thought was that the family that had sold the ranch to us had changed their mind; they didn't want to move. I was flabbergasted, frustrated, and moving quickly to extreme agitation. What in the hell was going on? It was extremely unprofessional of the Realtor. He got a damn good commission, and he moved a property that had been on the market a while because of the location. Joyce was curious but not frustrated. She laughed a little. It broke the tension and I broke down and chuckled. With all the contents of the house still there we had nowhere to put our contents for the house. I'd rented the truck for twenty-four hours. There was a penalty for breaking the contract. It cost more to keep the truck an extra day without a contract than it did to contract the truck, commitment to other customers I suppose. I was in a jackpot on what was supposed to be a happy day, a day I might look back upon for years, the day I took possession of my ranch.

Stay cool, Joyce said. It's no big deal.

With the rental truck in the laneway and Joyce by my side, I took out my cell phone and called the Realtor. I told him what was going on. He was incredulous.

Really? he said.

Everything, I said. Even the television.

The kitchen? he asked.

Everything, I repeated.

He suggested we go for lunch, see a movie, kill a few hours in nearby Buckeye, or go for a drive — anything to kill some time — and he seemed convinced he could settle the problem by the evening. It was about eleven o'clock in the morning.

Joyce and I did just that. We left the rental truck and drove in our car, went to town, had a nice lunch, saw a movie — *Mission Impossible* with Tom Cruise — did a little window-shopping, then, early in the evening, we returned to the ranch.

Upon entering the home, I was surprised to see that the entire house had been cleaned out, which was no small job. I was frankly amazed that the Realtor was able to pull it off. By that time it was late in the evening and we decided that we were going to start moving the contents of the rental truck into the ranch in the morning. We brought in a mattress to sleep on the floor, but, before I went to bed, I decided to survey the property. I turned on the outdoor light for the backyard and walked out under the desert sky. When I looked down, I was astounded to see all of the contents of the house — the refrigerator, the washing machine and dryer, every piece of furniture, all the utilities and appliances from the kitchen counter, mixers and blenders, everything that had been in the house — in the dry in-ground pool. It was a truly perplexing circumstance. If the old owners of the ranch, or someone acting on their behalf, had come to the house to move the contents, why did they put it all in the pool? It would have been easier and less distance to walk with the heavy utilities and furniture to a truck. Whatever cost the labor and the truck would have been could easily have been offset by selling the furniture at a local second-hand store or giving it to friends or family. There was absolutely no rhyme or reason for everything that had been in the house being in the pool.

I went in the house and got Joyce.

That doesn't make any sense, she said upon seeing the pool full of expensive house contents.

I know, right? I said.

There's thousands of dollars of appliances and furniture, she said.

Close to ten thousand or more, I added, as the two of us stared at the pool like we were hypnotized by a car crash.

The only thing that came to my mind was that the Realtor had paid some unreliable labor to do the task. I called him back. He assured me that this was not the case. He had been unable to make an arrangement to remove the contents of the house.

Well, who the hell did this, then? I asked sarcastically.

I have no idea, the Realtor replied.

Did you get a hold of the old owners? I asked.

No, the Realtor said. Their contact number is no longer in service.

This is really weird, I said.

You have some really nice stuff for free, he said.

I have my own stuff, I said. What am I supposed to do with a pool full of furniture and appliances?

John, he said. It's not my problem anymore. You paid cash for the house. It's your house, your problem.

It was an enormous task getting the stuff out of the pool. I had to go to a tool rental depot and get a winch. I'd never operated a winch before. It took some time to get the hang of it. I would put the really heavy, cumbersome items, like the refrigerator, stove, and washer and dryer, on a dolly and wheel them to the end of the laneway. I was pissed off. It was a lot of work. I didn't put everything out in one day. I put it out in drips and drabs and let people drive by and pick it up at their own pace. It took about three weeks to get rid of all the contents of the pool. To this day it remains a mystery. I have no idea who did it. It defies logic. It would have been more logical to just take the stuff. Most of it was in excellent condition. A salvage company would have loved to get their hands on it. In hindsight, I should have just called a salvage company or a second hand or vintage store owner, explained the situation, listed the contents of the house, the brand names of the appliances, and told them it was all in great condition. They would have sent a truck with six guys in thirty minutes. Instead, I left it to the Realtor, who really didn't care. He made his commission. There was nothing left in it for him.

It took about a week to get everything the way we wanted it in the house. It was a tonne of work. I did all the heavy lifting myself. The awkward stuff I moved with a dolly. The good thing about this home was that it was a ranch house — all one floor — so there were no stairs to lift things up.

Joyce persisted with her *bad feeling* about the ranch. The pool fiasco did nothing to change her gut feeling, the opposite; it made her more suspicious of the place, and it validated her intuition. Her entire particip- ipation in the project was to satisfy me, and I was extremely grateful. It's not that she was against the idea of a long commute to Phoenix, where she still worked in a clerical capacity at the Arizona headquar- ters of the FBI, but rather the particular ranch we bought. Looking back on it now, I Was a fool not to follow my wife's intuition. I was so pos- sessed by the idea of realizing my dream of living in a peaceful and quiet place, getting a few dozen horses, starting a dog kennel, running an animal shelter, and living the life I had been dreaming about for years, that I couldn't see what was going on around me, and I couldn't relate to what my wife was feeling.

The Man Who Killed Monsters

The experience with the contents of the house in the pool left me out of sorts. I kept my thinking to myself and didn't share it with Joyce. I don't know if I was just being paranoid, but it suddenly dawned on me that there were aspects of living in such a remote location that I had not accounted for, specifically safety. I bought a gun, a 357 Magnum. I had never been a big gun guy, but living in such a remote area, where police response might be quite some time, I decided it was prudent of me to have a weapon to protect myself and my wife. Little did I know back then that I would come to arm myself in ways that I had never imagined.

I have waited so long to tell this story in its entirety, and I didn't keep notes, a diary, or a journal of any kind, all of my recollections are *best guess*. With that said, sometime in our second month at the ranch I was home alone while Joyce was at work in Phoenix. I saw a man come off the road and begin walking up my long dirt laneway. Right away I knew there was something off about him. He was about five feet-nine inches tall, and he wore a military-style shirt with the sleeves cut off over a t-shirt. He had on a very well worn pair of jeans that looked as though they hadn't been washed in some time. A very worn pair of lace black boots adorned his feet. He had long gray hair parted in the middle — sort of like Willy Nelson — and somewhere between a one and a two-week salt and pepper beard over very gaunt cheeks.

I put the gun into the back of my pants and walked out of the house to meet him on the laneway. As I got closer to him, I could see an intensity to his eyes, something I had come to equate with the many psychotics I met in my counseling practice. His teeth were in horrible condition, yellow and broken, marking him as someone who had lived rough for a while, years maybe, but what caught my attention most was the well used twenty-four inch machete he was carrying in his hand. He didn't appear to have a scabbard for it. A man walking around with a machete was not out of place in Rainbow Valley, but a man walking around holding a machete was unusual.

It made me tense up in the way I used to feel when I was walking around my neighborhood in Evanston, as though anything could happen, as though I had to be prepared for immediate and spontaneous violence. We both came to a stop around the midpoint of the hundred-yard laneway, ten feet between us, squared off like a couple of gunfighters cautiously studying each other. I spoke first.

Can I help you?

I live here, he said.

Excuse me? I asked. I tried not to be rude or too incredulous because I didn't know what the guy was talking about.

He pointed up with the machete off to the distance, stating he lived there.

I took a glance behind me. I assumed he meant the storage shack about twenty-five fifty yards from the main house. I'd already taken a look inside it. I didn't see the makings of any kind of squat for this homeless man. I had the sense that he was a veteran. In any case, I was extremely tolerant of him.

I'm sorry, I said. I don't have an arrangement with you. Did the previous occupants allow you to live on the land? Did you help out around here or something?

He then said something that made my whole body tighten up.

I kill the monsters.

I don't know why, but even thinking back about this all those years ago, makes me uncomfortable. I quickly became impatient with the man.

Look, I don't know what arrangement you had with the previous owners of this ranch, but I don't want you living here.

He sort of cold-cocked me with a thousand-yard stare and simply said, You're going to regret that.

Then he turned around and walked away as he had come.

Between the man with the machete in my laneway and the entire contents of the house being put in the pool, I still did not connect with Joyce's intuition about the place. I guess I should have seen it. It could not have been a stronger forewarning by the law of circumstance and synchronicity. The only thing missing was the crazy old man from the *Friday the 13th* movie franchise, warning the teenagers not to go to Camp Blood.

Chapter 2

Phone Lines

In keeping with my home defense motif, I decided we needed a land-line telephone. Both Joyce and I had cell phones but a landline was added security. One of the odd little things I noticed when looking at the house was an unusually large number of telephone lines. I counted around thirty the first time we saw the house. There were so many things to discuss that first visit that I didn't think to ask about them. I remember thinking to myself: I could do anything with this house, any kind of business that involved multiple phone lines. I forgot to ask the Realtor why there were so many phone lines. There were a million and one other questions our first viewing.

I called Southwest Bell, my local telephone company for landlines, and I requested a phone line. The person I spoke to assured me that the service person would be out the following day. However, they weren't able to narrow it down to less than a four-hour block of time, which meant that I had to put aside a whole bunch of time to be close to the house when I had other things to do.

The first appointment came and went and no service person showed up at the house. I was a little irritated but I didn't become angry. I waited until the end of the work day, and I called Southwest Bell again, and I spoke to a different person in the service department. I explained the situation. The the customer service representative apologized pro-fusely and assured me that the next available day, three days further into the week, a service person would be out to install the landline.

Three days later, on the appointed day, in the four-hour block of time, I patiently waited at the house, and once again no service person turned up. This second time I was not so gracious when I called Southwest Bell. When I got the customer service representative on the phone I said: Look, this is getting outrageous. You have promised me twice now that a service person would come by the house. In each instance I waited for hours and put away half of my day and no service person came to install my landline.

Once again the customer service representative apologized profusely, but the second time it wasn't enough for me. I asked to speak to the manager of the division. I waited on the phone a couple minutes before I was transferred to another line. A relatively pleasant female voice picked up the phone and said, can I help you?

I told my story for the second time. I had put aside two different half days to wait for a Southwest Bell service person to come by the house and do the most remedial thing that the phone company does, install a landline, and twice my installer was a no-show. The manager of the division asked for my address. I gave it and then waited. I could hear activity on the other end of the phone, her fingers hitting the keyboard, stop, fingers hitting the keyboard, over and over for about five minutes. I assumed she was reading reports on my address from the database. I guess the ranch had quite a history with Southwest Bell, that would explain the thirty landlines coming into the house.

What was different this time was the manager of customer service didn't brush me off or give me a nonsensical excuse. Her voice changed. It was kind of an *I'm going to level with you voice*, not the normal pleasant happy customer service voice with which they had been trained to speak to customers.

She said, Sir, the problem is that our installers are subcontractors or independent contractors, if you will, and, as such, we can't really force them to do anything. Our work orders come up and they go out over the system and we get confirmations. If a service rep takes the work order we have no real way to follow-up on whether or not they are committed to going out and fulfilling it.

I thought her explanation was a little ridiculous so I said, That's no way to run a business.

She agreed, but added that the business model had never really had problems like this before. Their model operated extremely well. The problem, she stated, was my address. My house had *something of a reputation* and none of the contractors wanted to go out. They may have just glanced at the work order, not realizing it was *the house* and accepted the contract to go and install the phone line, but, on the contracted day to fulfill the work order, upon taking out the map book, looking more closely at the address, and finally realizing where it was, they didn't fulfill the order.

I tried to take this all in calmly. My house had a bad reputation, so much so Southwest Bell installers didn't want to come over, but somehow my Realtor didn't know this? I didn't know this? What did Southwest Bell installers know that I didn't?

I asked. What kind of a *reputation*?

Strange, she confided. Your house has a strange reputation.

Can you be a little more specific? I asked.

They're afraid, she said. They're scared to go to your house.

Scared of what? I asked.

The reputation, Mr. Edmonds.

Call me old-fashioned, but the word reputation for me has always applied to loose women and competent specialists.

Women got reputations in high school. A construction contractor who does home renovations gets a reputation as competent and reliable or untrustworthy. I had no idea what reputation meant in context to a house. The customer service manager assured me that the following week an installer would come by. She would see to it herself. I got her name and her word.

In her non-customer service voice, her *let's be frank with each other* voice, she told me that the subcontractors were afraid to come out to my house because bad things had happened at the property. I asked what she meant. She wouldn't elaborate on what things had happened on my property. She asked for two hours to sort things out and said she would call me back. I agreed.

When the two hours came and went, I called Southwest Bell back. I tried to get the same woman but nobody had heard of a woman who worked at Southwest Bell by her name. I literally could not believe what was going on in my life in that first month and a half at the ranch. Between the lunatic showing up with the machete and all of the contents of the house put into the pool, this was starting to become annoying. It was like an inside story everybody knew except me. It was extremely frustrating. I did not have the patience or temperament to call Bell Southwest back again that day. I terminated all contact with the company and decided to just let myself cool down for a few days and try to figure out what was going on.

Lo and behold, the next day a little white cube van with the logo of a telephone company pulled into my laneway. Now remember, the woman I had spoken to *frankly* from Bell Southwest, the woman nobody knew at the company, the woman who had not called back in two hours to give me an appointment, that woman had somehow managed to secure an appointment for me the next day. I was perplexed and satisfied at the same time.

I watched this little fellow get out of the truck and nervously look around the property. — five feet and six inches, thick, black-rimmed glasses, a well manicured mustache, a long-sleeved white shirt, toolbox in hand — like he was trying to scout for vicious dogs or something. After fifteen or twenty seconds to satisfy himself that nothing was going to attack him right there in the laneway, he shuffled up to the doorway.

I went outside and introduced myself as the man who had requested the phone service. I'll never forget the look on his face. He looked like he'd just seen a ghost. He nodded his head and accepted my extended hand. I turned and he followed me into the house. He looked all around when we entered the house. There was a skittishness about him. I pointed to where I wanted the phone line in the kitchen. He nodded and opened his toolbox on the kitchen counter.

I felt I should say something, so I looked at him and said, I bought this house a couple months ago. I don't know anything about the property, its past, or its reputation. I understand that there was some concern about coming out here for a service call?

My voice and what I said seemed to calm him. He looked at me with a more relaxed expression and said, So you don't know any of the history of this property?

I assured him I did not. For the next ninety minutes I was given an extraordinary history lesson. The subcontractor that Southwest Bell had sent was in fact a resident of Buckeye himself and knew Rainbow Valley. By the time he was done his history lesson I understood the reputation of my house.

14700 S Tuthill Road

The main house on the ranch was built in 1977. The land was purchased by a man who quietly built the house himself as a surprise for his wife. When the house was finished and he brought his wife out to see it, she took one look at the land and the house and said that she would never live there. If he forced her to live there she would divorce him. The man was somewhat devastated because he had worked for some months and spent considerable money on the land and the construction of the ranch, all in an effort to please his wife. He didn't understand her response. Whatever went on in the marriage, they did end up living on the ranch for a short period of time, but the woman, true to her word, divorced him.

After this unfortunate circumstance, the property was sold to an off-track betting organization, which explained all the phone lines in the house. But that wasn't enough. They extended their business into prostitution and ran a brothel on the premises as well. This went on for quite a while, until the whole thing was shut down and the law in Maricopa County was changed making off-track betting illegal.

The *Sons of Gestapo* are another little mystery from the area. They are alleged to have derailed the *Sunset Limited* Amtrak train in the middle of the desert, *alleged* because it was never proven. Several notes purporting to be from the Sons of Gestapo were found near the crash. There was a clear anti-government message, especially toward the FBI and ATF.

At the time nobody had heard of the Sons of Gestapo, and it would be fair to say that right-wing extremist groups were well monitored by the federal government. Remember, this is shortly after the Oklahoma City bombing, Waco, Texas, and Ruby Ridge. Bill Clinton was in the White House and Janet Reno was the Attorney General for the United States. There was little tolerance for fringe groups of a white Christian variety, and an atmosphere of domestic terrorism had emerged under Reno. Crazy crackers with guns and Bibles who wanted to live communally almost immediately qualified for government surveillance.

The entire affair stinks of some kind of a cover-up, and many analysts have given their opinion that a right-wing extremist group did not perform this derailment. It had all the hallmarks of a government job, a false flag. As hard as it might be for people to believe, certain cells of our federal government can do some very bad things to push forward agendas. It's part of the world we live in.

The only piece of first-hand evidence to be released, a note purportedly written by the Sons of Gestapo, was given to an independent researcher named Paul Craig Roberts after he wrote a scathing rebuke of the government's white terrorism hypothesis. It reads as follows with no corrections.

Indictment of the ATF and the FBI

Before dawn the women awoke to say their morning prayers. The women slept upstairs. They lit their kerosene lamps because the electricity had been turned off by the FBI. After observing lights in all the upstairs windows, the FBI ordered the teargas bombardment. Afterwards only two upstairs windows were lit. The location of each was recorded. Over the next few hours, ventilation holes were poked into the walls. These holes made the fire burn very much faster. Otherwise the fire department would have had time to put out the fire before the women and children died in the flames. At noon the light from the two kerosene lamps was obscured by bright sunlight. Everyone had forgotten about them except the man who carried their locations written on a scrap of paper in his pocket. He ordered the tank drivers where to crash through. Guess under which two windows. He ordered them to raise their guns. As they backed out, the guns were lowered. The video tape shows clearly the floor being raised by the tank a foot and a half. Guess what happened to the kerosene lamps in the rooms above the tanks. A minute afterwards black smoke started to pour out of the windows where the lamps had burned. This is the normal time needed for a kerosene fire to build up.

Who is policing the ATF, FBI, state troopers, county sheriffs and local police? What federal law enforcement agency investigates each and every choke hold killing committed by a police officer? each and every beating of a drunk whether or not a passerby videotapes it? each and every shooting of a police officer's wife who knows too much about drug kickbacks? each and every killing at Ruby Ridge? The Gestapo accounts to no one. This is not Nazi Germany. All these people had rights. It is time for an independent Federal agency to police the law enforcement agencies and other government employees.

Sons of the Gestapo

SOG

The Sons of Gestapo were living at my ranch. They were the owners after the off-track betting and brothel operation. The Southwest Bell subcontractor told this story with some zeal. He was something of an enthusiast. The alleged militia, which nobody around Buckeye really believed was a militia, was pinned in the ranch by a federal assault team that had come to either question or arrest them in the derailment. The story goes that the Sons of Gestapo would not be questioned. A shootout ensued and several of them were killed. More blood on the ranch.

When I was told this story the Internet was not what it is today. Several times in the last ten years I've tried to investigate the story more fully, but there's precious little information aside from the original press reporting, much of which doubts the legitimacy of the militia group. There is absolutely no mention of a massacre at my ranch, in fact, there is absolutely no follow-up to what happened to the Sons of Gestapo.

In the course of writing this book, Bruce MacDonald called the Maricopa County Sheriff's Department and spoke to the records division. They told them that they couldn't help him, but suggested that he call one of the divisions of the Sheriff's Office, the one closest to the ranch, suggesting an older sheriff's deputy might be able to give some information if they had been on the force long enough to remember the shootout.

The day that Bruce called the sheriff's department, I came home an hour after he had called them. There were three vehicles from the Maricopa County Sheriff's Department on and around my property. One of them was parked right in my laneway. All the sheriff's deputies were out taking pictures. They didn't bother me or ask me any questions when I came home, however, the timing of three sheriff's deputies showing up on my property an hour after Bruce MacDonald called the Sheriff's Office to get information about the Sons of Gestapo cannot be ignored.

The most curious thing about the whole derailment and the involvement of the Sons of Gestapo is that the media continues to cover the story. PBS did a follow-up two years ago on the mystery of the derailment, which was never solved. The television show, *Unsolved Mysteries* with Robert Stack, did an episode on the derailment and the

Sons of Gestapo. Despite all of this coverage of the derailment, there is absolutely no follow-up anywhere online or at the Maricopa County Sheriff's Department, of what happened to the Sons of Gestapo. That they were living at my ranch is not in question. I've met countless Buckeye residents who confirmed what the telephone line installer told me. Yet the media has no account of a shootout at the ranch between the Sons of Gestapo, the ATF, the FBI, and the Maricopa County Sheriff's Department, despite the fact that there are casualties numbering four to six and a complete evacuation of a group of people who had been living a communal lifestyle at the ranch. Even more curiously, nowhere in the annals of white supremacy, including prison culture in America, is there any real knowledge of the Sons of Gestapo. The Ku Klux Klan know nothing about them. The Aryan Brotherhood knows nothing about them. Nobody has ever heard of them. And just like that, they disappeared off the face of the earth after they were smeared with responsibility for the derailment absent any conclusion to the investigation by the local, state, or federal authorities.

After the alleged Sons of Gestapo massacre, a Mexican family bought the ranch. The telephone installer didn't have all the details on how many people were in the family. They started a cattle operation and ran it successfully for a few years. They specialized in veal. On the day of the high school graduation for their son, he put a shotgun in his mouth and blew his head off. More blood on the ranch. As I listened to the Southwest Bell installer, I started to imagine that the earth itself on the ranch preferred blood to water.

When he was done his long yarn, I looked at him and said, What can I do?

He looked back at me and said, I would cancel the sale and sue the Realtor and get my money back.

I told him I paid cash and that wasn't going to happen. He looked away and had nothing more to say to me.

Chapter 3

Wild Horses and Strange Lights

To the best of my recollection, those were the three things that were most strange in our first few months at the new ranch: the entire previous owner's house contents in the swimming pool, the man who killed monsters, and the strange but amusing history lesson by the Southwest Bell serviceman.

Looking back on it now, these two decades and some later, I am forced to admit that Joyce's intuition was razor-sharp. Much like the wife of the man who built the original building and guest house, my wife never quite settled into the ranch in Rainbow Valley.

Our days were very different, Joyce and I. I would wake up every morning at around 4:30 AM, prepare breakfast and coffee for Joyce, while she got ready for work, then she came out to the kitchen, ate her breakfast with me, and left for work. She had a long commute into Phoenix, another incidental tax I put upon her, another sacrifice she made for me. The work at the FBI was satisfying for her, and we needed the money to keep our lives going. I had paid for the ranch, and I was staying home at the time, burned out from years of social work with drug addicts, homeless people, army veterans, and a host of other misshapen people who had been deformed by life's vicissitudes.

I had four pairs of male-female Rottweilers when Joyce and I moved to Rainbow Valley. I'd always loved the breed, and with the ranch I was able to give them the perfect life. After Joyce went to work every morning, I would take the dogs out and let them run around for a bit. I would feed and water them and give them all their individual attention. If there were any errands to be run in town, I would choose one of the couples, throw them in the truck with me, and go do my errands with them. The rest of the time they were in the kennel. My love of animals has always been a big part of my life, and it was also a big part of why I wanted to get a ranch.

A lot of time was spent tinkering around the ranch, fixing fences, doing small repairs, a little bit of interior redesigning, and general maintenance. There was fence to be built, horse gear to be oiled and polished, stables to be cleaned, and a whole host of things too numerous to list here — you get the point. There was always something to keep me busy, always some improvement to be made. People who own farms get like this. It's like maintaining a home just much larger. Throw the animals and their shelters and habitations into the mix and you have non-stop work, none of it life and death, none of it absolutely necessary, but all of it strangely comforting, the work of the soul one might say, the fulfillment of the old Protestant adage that idle hands are the work of the devil.

I became more curious about the hundreds of square miles of empty desert and red rock mountains around me. I had a Jeep four by four, and I decided to do a little off-road exploration. I would drive in any direction over the dry, barren land of the desert, which I found most beautiful at dawn and dusk because of the ribbons of color in the sky and the sun coming up or going down behind the mountains. It's a certain kind of person who finds contentment in barren places. The desert has always been a place for hard-nosed people. I imagine it's similar at the North Pole, the commonality being a simple and endless pallet for the vision, one a yellow-orange sandy forever and the other an endless field of ice.

I don't remember exactly when it was that I started to notice the lights in the sky. Arizona has always been a Mecca for the New Age movement and a certain kind of person taken with the unexplained. These are the people who migrated to Arizona from other parts of the United States and the world, that's not to diminish the flocking of Canadian retirees looking for something different from Florida, or the people born and raised in the state and accustomed to its high strangeness, but mixed in with them are these spiritual migrants, these seekers, these imaginative zombies enraptured by the siren song of the mysterious.

The only way I can properly describe the lights that I saw in the sky is to say that they seemed to be alive. They seemed to be conscious, self-directed, and they could do things lights shouldn't be able to do. The predominant color of the lights was orange, but there were other colors as well. They could move across the sky faster than anything in nature or anything that human beings have made to travel in the sky, including fighter jets. I did learn early on that there was a military base twelve miles away on the other side of the mountains, but these lights were not any kind of military craft. From my vantage in the Jeep, they looked like fireflies, however, the distance they were away from me in the sky and off on the horizon would mean that their actual size was much larger than a firefly. I won't even try and guess how big the lights were. I would watch them dance around in the sky and move across the horizon in a second. Sometimes it seemed to me that they could just disappear and reappear miles away in an instant. They were hypnotic to watch, not solely by their movement and the oddity of what they might be, but just in the general sort of way the human mind will go into a trance when it is captured by the rarefied emotions of wonder and awe. Put simply, they left me slack-jawed.

I remember my wife getting home from work and me telling her about what I had seen out in the desert, which made me look like a damn fool.

Are you sure that's what you saw? she'd ask.

It's a curious aspect of human beings, our nature, and our behavior, that we disregard anything outside the normal human experience that we have not experienced ourselves. I suppose you could call that sane, but in another way it seems like a limitation. Anybody who has not experienced the haunted house is skeptical about the entire notion of ghosts. Certainly, if you've never seen a Bigfoot you're going to remain skeptical, and, going by the reaction of my wife in those early months at Stardust Ranch, the same goes for lights in the sky that move in a way that no object made by man can move. Of course this was just the beginning of our sojourn at Stardust Ranch. My wife would join me soon enough as an experiencer.

Adopting Horses

One of the natural treasures I discovered in the desert was a horse population. They were thin and malnourished Food and water were hard to come by in that barren and scrub land. The horses were not wild. I don't know where they came from. Perhaps various ranchers had let them go into the desert to die, not knowing what else to do with them, and not wanting them anymore. They were skittish and reserved when I would drive close to them in the Jeep. My heart opened, and I decided that I wanted to help these horses. So I went into Buckeye, and I bought some hay, and I filled a couple fifty-gallon barrels with water, and I put the hay and the water in a trailer, and I towed the trailer off-road into the desert where I had seen the horses. They were able to smell the hay right away and came in completely devoid of the fear and hesitation they'd had when I showed up without food. Once they got used to being fed and watered it was no problem at all to get them to follow me back to the ranch. I drove slowly with a little bit of hay in the trailer and some two dozen horses ambled behind me and came back to my ranch. I easily corralled them and took it upon myself to restore their health and make them useful and loved animals. Some of them needed to see a veterinarian, so I called the vet and he came out and examined my animals. I told him where I had found the animals and he said that, in fact, it was ranchers who let them go. What a sad state of affairs when a horse came to such a state. I believe what Cormac McCarthy, the great American novelist believes, that a horse has a nearly human soul.

The animal aspect of running a ranch was beginning to fulfill itself with the discovery of the horses. With a little help from my neighbors and a little bit of research, I was able to bond with the horses, settle them down, and get them in a trusting relationship with me. I was very happy with this. I had come with the eight dogs and I wanted to get more, and I knew that I wanted to get horses, but I didn't know how I would go about doing that. I could always go to auctions and buy horses, but that seemed a little bit expensive, and I didn't even know what I was looking for. The fact that I could just get into my Jeep, go out into the desert, befriend wild or abandoned horses by bringing a little bit of feed and water, then have them follow me back to the ranch and go into a corral, was the most pleasant surprise of my new experience at the ranch.

Luke Air Force Range

Just on the other side of the mountain was the Luke Air Force Range, which later came to be named, The Barry Goldwater Air Force Range. I would soon find out that it was common for the government to use the military range as an excuse for reported lights like the ones I saw regularly. They would tell people who saw the lights in the area that they were just flares and were part of military drills. The range was used for fighter jet bombing practice. It is true that there were lights and there were night lights associated with night drills, but that didn't come anywhere close to explaining what was going on with the lights in the sky. There were also times during the day when I was out in my Jeep that I saw fighter jets engaging lights, but they were no match for the fast-moving lights which could turn one hundred and eighty degrees at unbelievable speeds.

During these first few months on the ranch, I got to know some of the neighbors and some of the people in town where I did business. There was a kind of *hush* about people in this part of Arizona. I don't know how else to describe it. If you were an outsider, it was like you had come to some kind of haunted village, and, if you didn't figure out it was haunted on your own, nobody wanted to be the one to tell you, so when you spoke to people, especially when you hinted at things like the lights in the sky, there was a hesitation before they would get into any kind of dialogue with you.

People were wary of the military base on the other side of the mountain. They certainly didn't accept the explanations given by the government for the strange lights in the sky. I also began to get a sense of other things that were not quite right in the valley. People would hint at things — bumps in the night, disturbing animal mutilations, people leaving town quickly, and veiled references to my property — but they wouldn't come right out and tell you anything until they knew you could handle it. I got it. I was going through the same thing with Joyce. I'd walked into a place that was like a *Twilight Zone* episode, or the entire television show in one county. Welcome to Arizona. In that kind of atmosphere people retreated into themselves. If you asked about something like the lights in the sky while in the hardware store, you might get a polite affirmation — yeah, there were lights in the sky in that part of Arizona — but no deep conversation about what might really be going on, nothing beyond agreement with your observation.

There is absolutely no doubt in my mind that the US Military and Government are completely aware of the extraterrestrial presence in our country and the world and that they are having engagements all the time. Why they persist in the *see nothing-know nothing* public narrative is a mystery to me. They've been using the training drill excuse for the lights in Arizona for decades now. The people who have seen the lights know by their own experience that they are not related to any military technology, and it sows doubt between the governed and the government, like the phony Sons of Gestapo story they tried to force-feed people. It had more holes than a termite infested tree. The flare excuse is the most ridiculous. If they were in fact flares that were causing the lights in the sky then there would be a lot more fires in the desert. The desert is extremely dry and there's a lot of combustible material out there. You can start a desert fire just throwing a cigarette down on the ground.

Goldwater and Arizona

Arizona has been a part of the UFO narrative since it came into existence. Extraterrestrials do not enter the human narrative in any significant way until after the Second World War. I had been living in Glendale before I bought the ranch. I knew the stories. I was really just not a UFO guy. It's not that I dismiss them, they just weren't a great draw for me. I'd always thought of UFO people as having nothing else going on in their life, people drawn into a fantasy world, like the Dungeons & Dragons people, or comic book people, or people who watch too many movies. I'd always had too much going on in my life to be that guy. Nonetheless, it was impossible to move to Arizona and not hear about UFOs. I didn't know at that time in late 1996 and early 1997 that I was going to be drawn into the UFO world and become something of a spokesperson for it.

There is an irony in the air force base being named Barry Goldwater. Goldwater, a five-time US senator from Arizona, was one of the most outspoken government officials about the possibility of a UFO cover-up by the government.

In 1978, Goldwater said in an interview:

The subject of UFOs has interested me for some long time. About ten or twelve years ago I made an effort to find out what was in the building at Wright-Patterson Air Force Base where the information has been stored that has been collected by the Air Force, and I was understandably denied this request. It is still classified above Top Secret.

In 1988 he was asked on *Larry King* if he believed the government was withholding information on extraterrestrial life. He responded:

I certainly believe in aliens in space. They may not look like us, but I have very strong feelings that they have advanced beyond our mental capabilities... I think some highly secret government UFO investigations are going on that we don't know about — and probably never will unless the Air Force discloses them.

When you move to Arizona you hear the UFO lore over casual conversations with the residents. The first really good picture of a UFO was taken in Arizona by a guy named William Rhodes on July 7th, 1947. Rhodes went through the same kind of discrimination that officialdom is want to do when somebody in the civilian world has hard proof of a UFO. Much like the Bob Lazar case from Area 51, Rhodes had a relationship with the military industrial complex that they wanted to deny. He claimed that he worked on some military projects related to cutting-edge technology, and that he had the equivalent of a PhD. Rhodes himself wrote:

Additionally, after being thoroughly investigated by the FBI, I was issued top-secret status. Not even my wife was to know. The creation was a method of neutralizing the earth's magnetic field in ships. Not a single ship or sailor was lost to magnetic mines during the war's remainder. One day, my boss summoned me to his office and explained: "We have a total absence of degree'd doctorates, and having already passed requirements, you have been selected to receive a Ph.D in Physics. The degree would be known by the nickname"90 Day Wonder", and my work would not be disrupted to gain it.

This revoking of top secret clearance and complete disavowal once a person goes public with material related to UFOs is standard operating procedure in the UFO world. It's the same story with Bob Lazar and Area 51. There was the alleged crash of an alien craft in Roswell, New Mexico, the neighboring state. The commonality was the desert and the time. There has been a lot of nuclear testing in Nevada, and the desert of America's southwest seem to be some kind of nodal point for flying objects that can not be identified. Rhodes had his negatives taken by an unidentified government agency that never returned them.

The next big event in UFO lore for Arizona was an alleged crash of an alien craft in a place called Dreamy Draw. It happened three months after the Roswell crash and the UFO was allegedly buried under a damn which still operates to this day. Then comes the first recorded abduction, Travis Walton in 1975. He was in a truck with a half-dozen other men and they saw a UFO. Walton got out of the truck and walked over. According to the other men, a beam of blue green-light came out and knocked Walton unconscious and pulled him into the craft. His co-workers drove away hastily. Walton was gone for five days, reappearing naked and traumatized by the side of a highway, claiming he saw the craft take off, and telling a tale of brown-eyed aliens that had abducted him. He later wrote a book called *Fire in the Sky* that documented the whole experience, and it has become mandatory reading for the cult of UFO aficionados. A movie was subsequently made.

By far the most known UFO story in Arizona takes place shortly after I bought the ranch, and here I am talking about the Phoenix Lights in 1997, witnessed by thousands of people in the state and recorded by media outlets. And once again the government gave little information or credulity to the idea that this was a UFO experience. They prefer to talk about weather and gas in the sky or any other kind of pseudoscientific reason that might take away from the credulity of UFOs and extraterrestrials in the human experience.

Fiction and Non-Fiction

Human beings usually engage difficult topics first through fiction. A human being will contemplate anything that's put in front of them in a Jules Verne novel, a comic book, or a TV series. As I went about Arizona, trying to find answers for what was happening on my ranch in those first few months, I ran up against tight-lipped government agencies, a sheriff's office under Joe Arpaio that treated me like I might be mentally insane, and neighbors who just sort of looked away for the most part when the topic was brought up. Don't get me wrong, there are always exceptions. There are people willing to talk about anything, and there were people in the area who had experienced events similar to me.

Through the entire time that I was trying to come to an understanding of what was going on in Rainbow Valley, and specifically at my ranch, people were enraptured with what was I believe the number one show on television at that time, *The X-Files*. In the show, the FBI has a secret division for paranormal cases. A male and a female FBI officer team up together, one a believer, because his sister was abducted by aliens, and the other a hardcore skeptic and rationalist in the form of a medical doctor. It's a tried-and-true device for using difficult material to filter through a logical mind. The believer was Agent Mulder, played by David Duchovny. The skeptic was Agent Scully, played by Gillian Anderson.

I felt like a third agent in that FBI division called the X-Files. Everywhere I went I was stonewalled and told that what I was trying to tell people was crazy. The truth is — this has taken time to understand over the years — after witnessing dozens of people come and stay at the ranch, and their various reactions to the phenomenon at the ranch (keeping in mind that there were people who visited here and experienced nothing) is that fiction, the suspension of disbelief but the failure to engage a full reality, is a modality of consciousness by which we assimilate material that's outside our normal understanding of reality.

Some people have a buffer language to use, like calculus. The scientists can move into hypothetical regions of reality using calculus and forego the state of fiction or disbelief. But in a certain sense even the math keeps it at bay, keeps it from that part of their minds that truly understands something to be real at an experiential level. It's one thing to figure out mathematically the theory of anti-gravity and to levitate a small disc, as it is rumored the scientists at Area 51 did, but it's another thing altogether to get into a disc and fly off into space.

Human beings have been grappling with the idea of life in the solar system, the galaxy, and the universe for about a hundred and twenty years. The human imagination really doesn't get stoked until Jules Verne. His speculative fiction allowed the human imagination to go places it had not been before. He took us into the ocean with *20,000 Leagues Under the Sea*, and he took us to the center of the earth with

Journey to the Center of the Earth. And then the idea of life on other planets is placed in front of us with Orson Welles' *War of the Worlds.* Originally it was a radio broadcast. It was so effective and compelling that people were put into a panic and preparing for an alien invasion.

The next big engagement of the human imagination as it pertains to life from other planets is *The Day the Earth Stood Still.* There are many rumors about this film. For decades now it has been suggested that this was a way of telling the public about President Eisenhower's secret treaty with aliens. In any event, the film had a very profound impact on the public. Coincidentally, both *War of the Worlds* and *The Day the Earth Stood Still* have been remade in the last twenty years. *War of the Worlds* was remade by Steven Spielberg with Tom Cruise in the center role, and this time it was a film and not a radio production. The *Day the Earth Stood Still* was remade with Keanu Reeves. It's almost as though the human imagination is being examined for its willingness and its ability to accept the idea that life from other planets have visited earth.

As you can well imagine, I have a very different perspective on all of these things. I've been forced to look long and deep into the phenomenon of extraterrestrial life due to my experiences at the ranch in Rainbow Valley, Arizona. It's my belief that alien life has always been here. Alien life is both negative and positive. Just like we human beings, the world of alien races has extremely negative and extremely positive actors.

Chapter 4

Disquiet

Somewhere around the sixty or ninety day mark in the home I became aware of a disquieting presence. I didn't know what it was at first. It affected my mood. I would find myself very angry all the time. I didn't express it around Joyce. I carried it around inside of me. I didn't know what it was. I started to feel the way I had felt when I grew up in Evanston. I was raised in a very rough part of Illinois by parents who did not have a lot of money. I learned to be hyper-vigilant. That's how you survive where I was raised. You could not take your eye off the game for a second. Walking down the sidewalk you had to be aware of the people loitering a hundred yards ahead of you. Eye contact or lack thereof was important. When you're a teenage kid walking around in my neighborhood eye contact for too long is a sign of aggression. But at the same time your eyes had to be working. This constant state of vigilance is what I noticed in myself when I was home alone on the ranch, especially when I was inside the house. It could go away for hours when I was doing chores or going into town, going to the feed store, the hardware store, stopping in for a coffee at the local coffee shop, chatting with locals in Buckeye, traveling around in the truck with a pair of the Rottweilers. All of these activities could abate that sense of vigilance. But the moment I got home, and I was alone in that house, it would return in very short time. There was a short grace I would have where the energy of my activity outside the house would still be in my mind, and I would be reminiscing about what I did, chuckling about little jokes I heard, and musing about conversations I had with people I'd bumped into during the day. But after that grace was gone, and my mind realized that I was alone in that house, the negativity would come on me again.

Because I was a trained counselor, I set up mental exercises to try to dismiss the tension. I tried to rationalize it. I would say to myself: John, why are you allowing yourself to feel tense? There's nothing to feel tense about here. I could manage it in some small measure, but, just like keeping your eyes open and peeled in the neighborhood in which I grew up, there was an equivalent form of psychological vigilance that I had to maintain to cope with being in the home. As you can well imagine, having put the majority of my life savings into the ranch, I was not enjoying it the way I thought I was going to enjoy it. Aside from the several small things already documented in this story, like the strange man with the machete who said he killed monsters, the inexplicable presence of all the contents of the house in the pool, and the lights I would see in the sky, both at night from the home, and during the day when I was out in the Jeep with the dogs, everything else was fairly normal, or lacking any phenomenon to suggest it was anything but normal. This left me to believe that everything that was going on was just in my head. Why would I believe anything else?

My mental discipline and psychological training aided me quite a bit in staying out of negative moods. But then something else started to happen. Small inconveniences would creep up all the time. I would go to use a tool and the electricity wouldn't work. There was no rational reason for why the electricity would not work. When I checked the fuses and the tool I was using, whether it was a skill saw or a drill, they were always in proper working condition, as was the electricity on the ranch. Often the situations would repair themselves without any tinkering on my part. It was almost as though some gremlin was at work.

Another thing that started to happen was that I misplaced a lot of things. I would lay my cell phone down, and, when I went to retrieve it a couple hours later, it would not be where I thought I had left it. Same thing with the car keys. Same thing with bills that had to be paid that I left on the kitchen table. This got to be such a phenomenon, that I thought I might be moving into early Alzheimer's. I mentioned it to Joyce and she said that she saw no evidence of it whatsoever. She, by the way, maintained her initial intuitive response to the ranch through-out this time, which was entirely negative. She wanted to leave. Let me be completely clear about that.

The phenomenon of the misplaced items became even more curious when they would reappear sometime later in exactly the same spot that I believed I originally left them and had already looked. So imagine you come home from ninety minutes of chores in town, you unload the truck of salt bags for the horses and other treats for the dogs and all the things that you bought in town, you do a quick walk around the property to make sure everything is okay, check on all the animals, go into the house, already having experienced the phenomenon of disappearing items, so you very consciously place your keys in a very specific spot, and then you go take a shower. Upon coming out of the bathroom some thirty minutes later, after shaving, washing my hair, and doing all of my grooming, I would return to the exact spot I consciously laid the keys, in full knowledge of the fact that I was misplacing a lot of things, and the keys would not be there.

At the risk of sounding paranoid, it was almost as though something was working against my psychological training and mental discipline to not go into negative spaces in my own mind. It was difficult. Try to put yourself in my position. You've already got this invisible disquiet that seems to be coming into your mind when you're alone in the house. You deal with that with a focused psychological treatment of yourself, and then the physical phenomenon of disappearing items to cause frustration begins recurring in your life. I started to get angry again. To be completely honest with you, I would sometimes have temper tantrums alone in the house — throw things around, kick things, punch the walls — always careful never to destroy anything. I didn't want Joyce to know that I was in a negative state of mind when I was home alone at the ranch, because then the inevitable conversation of why we were even staying at the ranch would commence.

I was the stalwart. I was the one who wanted to stay at the ranch, not Joyce, so I had to hold the line in this regard. It was incredibly difficult to maintain my mood and to stave off anger when there was already this invisible disquiet, this festering negativity in the house, almost like an odorless odor. There was almost a tangibility to it — couple this with the disappearing items and it became very difficult for me to maintain my composure.

When things started disappearing, I realized that I had to be more scientific about what was going on in the house when I was alone. I began to extract myself from the idea that this was all in my head, and I did what all rational people do — I documented. I began to notice that there was phenomenon associated with the sense of disquiet I had. The only thing I can compare it to is a change of pressure in the room. You might have experienced something like this in anticipation of a thunderstorm, or some similar climate related event, but I assure you it was physical. There was a distinct change of pressure in the room. Sometimes it would seem to get colder. These physical anomalies became my first documented symptoms of the disquieting presence in the house. Once I documented a change in the pressure and temperature in the room, I cast my gaze further afield. I noticed that before these events, these disquieting presences, there would be disruption and aberrant behavior among the animals. The horses would become agitated. The dogs would sometimes start fighting among themselves. Everything around me indicated that something preternatural was coming into my space, and all of this began with bad moods that I thought were just regrets about buying the ranch. As I was figuring all of this out, I did it the hard way. It wasn't until some months living at the ranch that I figured out that something was coming and going, something preternatural. Once I figured this out, it's almost as though whatever was there decided to express itself more freely given that I had accepted that it was there. It was like communication between us. It didn't reveal itself fully beyond just the pressure change and the behavior of the animals until I fully acknowledged in my own mind that it was real and it was not my imagination. From that point on, any time I would get angry, anytime I would let my emotions run away in a negative way, the environment would speak back to me in a paranormal way. Things would move around in the kitchen. Plates would fall off the counter and hit the floor. The refrigerator would rock back and forth, things like this, right on the periphery of paranormal and explainable, as though the entire drama was meant to drive me insane. From there it moved into the electronics. The television would come on by itself and go to its maximum volume. The stereo would turn on in the middle of the night. As time went on, both Joyce and I were acutely aware that there was something in the house. Because Joyce spent less time in the house than I did — she had a night job on top of her FBI office job that kept her away from the house from early in the morning till quite late at night — she was only at the house at night, and completely unaware of what I was dealing with. I tried to downplay the things like the TV and the stereo going on. I really didn't want to start to hear things like *I told you so*, and *we never should have bought this place*. I wanted to keep her shielded from what was going on. I wanted to keep it secret. In my own engagement with the negative forces at the ranch, I had been heartened by the changing pressure and the mood in the animals. These were points of reference for me to assure myself that I was not going crazy. The things that were happening were real. It was strange, but it could be explained or rationalized.

Dead Dog

The situation reached a pitch when I lost my favorite dog. We kept the dogs outside in dog crates in a large structure that was like a kennel. I spent time with the dogs everyday as I've already described. I can't remember when exactly I became so attached to the Rottweiler breed. It happened sometime in Glendale, Arizona. There really wasn't the space or climate to keep dogs like that in such numbers in Evanston. I've always had a very special relationship with animals. I've always felt really good with them around me, and I've always had one kind of a pet or another no matter where I lived. Later on we got a parrot at the house.

With Joyce having to be out of the house at a fairly early hour every day, the first thing I took care of every morning was her breakfast and coffee and we spent some time together before she left the house. It was after this that I would go and tend to the animals. First came the dogs, who I fed and watered and gave a little recreational time to, then came the horses, same thing, feeding and watering. On this particular day, as I watched Joyce drive off, I turned around to go out to the kennels and everything felt okay. I went out the back door and walked toward the Rottweilers, and even from some twenty-five yards away I could see that something was wrong.

One of the dog crates had been opened. I began to scan the terrain. Not too far from the dog crate, I saw what were the remains of my favorite Rottweiler. It was the first animal mutilation that I experienced on the property, and it was also the first experience with something that would come to represent the oppressive feeling and change of pressure that I had felt in the house. It had acted. I knew the moment I saw the dead dog it was the force in the house that was responsible. It wasn't my imagination, nor was I developing Alzheimer's and misplacing things constantly, nor were there any electrical problems in the house that would turn on the stereo or TV in the middle of the night. Now I knew all of these things were not accidents to begin with. It was all real, and it was becoming more aggressive. It seemed to be synced to my understanding of it, like it knew I was aware of it, beginning with the atmosphere changes when it showed up.

What was particularly disconcerting about the animal's death was the manner in which it had been killed. The carcass was completely flat, no thicker than a manhole cover. It was as though it had been run over by a steamroller. But there were no innards, no blood, no gore scattered about. It wasn't possible. There was also the crate to consider, something had to take the dog out of the crate. If you know anything about Rottweilers, the first thing you might be asking yourself right now is why didn't we hear anything in the middle of the night? There are eight dogs. One of them, my favorite, was taken out of his crate, desecrated and mutilated. I didn't hear any sound associated with the panic of the dog being killed, nor did I hear any barking from the seven companion dogs, who would have been in a state of extreme agitation knowing that one of their pack was being attacked and killed. My first emotional response was pure rage. I stomped around for some fifteen or twenty minutes just cursing and kicking the ground and yelling at the top of my lungs. Whatever did this had my full attention. The day that line was crossed, the day that my favorite dog was killed, was the day that I declared war on whatever was assaulting me in the ranch.

The death of the dog also marked the time for me to give full disclosure to Joyce. I couldn't live with this any longer, and I couldn't protect her from it any longer. The only sensible thing to do at that point was to tell her everything that had been going on, all of the things that I intuited, all of the little mood shifts during the day, the pressure and climate changes inside the house that came about suddenly, and all the bizarre little things that happened during the day when she was not there, like things cluttering around in the kitchen when nobody was there. With the death of the dog, Joyce and I had to accept the fact that we were living in a place that had phenomenon going on we knew absolutely nothing about.

When she got home that night, I took her outside with a flashlight and showed her the dead dog.

She was quiet for quite some time, a look of complete bewilderment on her face.

What could even do that? She said.

I have no idea, I answered.

Chapter 5

Weird and Violent

I can't overstate at this point the incredible sense of dread I had living at the ranch. By around month three, there was no denying that I was going through something heretofore unknown, and my life had changed. There was no more normal, no more idyllic ranch with tranquility, nothing more than fear and trepidation, a reality I had never fully contemplated, articulated in horror movies and novels, and fringe paranormal groups. Joyce was outside my understanding that first year. She hadn't been initiated like I had. She had the *force* working on her, the foul moods, the eruptions of anger. I knew what she was going through. I had been put through it first, being the one home at the ranch, morning to night, Monday to Friday.

The topic of moving came up again and again. Joyce affirmed her intuition. She had been right. It was time to accept our losses, put the property up for sale, find somebody as gullible as we were to buy it, and get the hell out of Dodge. I couldn't do it. I wanted to make Joyce happy. I did, however, I could not leave. I felt like a coward. I felt like I was being run off my home. Some ancient territorial defense consciousness awoke inside me. It's like a variation on the fight or flight impulse. I was not going to take flight. I was going to fight.

The violence did not stop with the dog. I had horses killed. It was always the same story. I would wake up in the morning to find the animal. The horses were killed in a manner equally bizarre but different than the dog. They were eviscerated. What was being done to the animals was beyond any comprehension. It would be hard to believe human beings did it even if a team of surgeons showed up in the middle of the night. The cuts and what was done to the bodies were not the product of human hands or instruments. The mystery of silence attended every animal slaughter. There was never any noise from any of the other animals. It didn't happen on a weekly or even a monthly basis. It just kept happening randomly over the years, always when enough time had passed so we forgot all about it.

Branded

The next thing to visit us at the ranch was the marking of our flesh, anomalous markings on the outside of our bodies, in some cases quite large, imprinted almost like brands, the way you would brand a horse or a cow. The truly odd thing about this was Joyce seemed unaware of it, which is very strange because most women are acutely aware of their physical appearance, but she seemed to not even notice that her body had been deformed in certain areas while she slept. It was a kind of disassociation, and at times it struck me almost as a kind of induced disassociation. To this day both of us look like we've been in horrible car crashes, with puncture marks and long scars and other deformities all over our bodies.

All of these markings took place in our sleep. Years later, when we knew what we were dealing with, they became more brazen. One time I was sitting on the ground in front of the television in the living room, the main room of the ranch, and I felt an intense heat on the back of my right calf, as though a red hot grill from a barbecue was pressed against the back of my calf. I screamed out in pain. I was branded. There were burn marks on the back of my calf. Nothing ever appeared in the room. Smoke had come off the back of my calf and the smell of burning flesh wafted through the air. But this was years into living at the ranch. In the beginning the force didn't reveal itself so convincingly. It was more subtle the first couple years, as though fully revealing itself was its trump card, to be played only when absolutely required.

Truth be told, things hadn't even started yet. As I think back on this, now living on the ranch just shy of a quarter-century, the only answer I can give is male pride. I had sunk all of my life savings or nearly all of my life savings into the ranch and I just could not envision a situation where I retreated, because I would take a huge loss selling the ranch under quick terms, and it wasn't something I was willing to face. I keep telling myself this. I've always told myself this. The truth is I don't know why I stayed.

Maybe I was addicted to how the ranch made me feel, special, chosen, entitled. Even with all the horror there was something profound about living at Stardust Ranch. Mixed in with the bad energy, the markings on our bodies, the dead animals, and the disappearing items, there were moments equal and opposite to the negative, a kind of pendulum swing into bliss and peace. I know how this all must sound, crazy, but I have lived it and I bare witness, as does Joyce. In spite of all I have told you, something made the ranch special.

I permanently changed my life and Joyce's life. I made decisions for both of us that have affected her enormously. We fought a lot in the first few year. We started to get into some humdingers, arguments and fights so fierce that if we had neighbors within a half mile we would have had the police called on us. The only thing that saved us from a 911 call from a concerned neighbor was probably all the open space around us. Dishes were thrown.

Expletives were commonplace at that time in our lives. Bursts of anger and vitriol in both of us were becoming the norm. We always made up after the fights, but we always fought again. At the root of it was this evil at the ranch that wanted us gone. I couldn't tell Joyce this. She wasn't ready to accept it in the first few years. She wasn't at the house day and evening. She came home late and slept. She woke up early and left again. On Saturdays we did chores and were out most of the day. Saturday evenings we usually watched a movie. Sundays we rode horses and went on long walks with the dogs. The weekends helped us reconnect. It was during the week we fought. The force at the ranch did this on purpose. It didn't reveal itself to Joyce the way it did with me. She was still at the first stage of the realization.

The bad moods in Joyce were the result of the unseen force. This was stage one. She was not having things disappear yet. She hadn't entered phase two. The dead dog was phase three, but Joyce didn't accept it as such because she hadn't graduated from phase two. The human mind fought the growing reality, the supernatural nature of it. This was all normal. Joyce believed human beings killed the dog. Without noticing the change in pressure, the slight difference in temperature that came on quickly, connecting the dog with the supernatural force was too far out.

She didn't have any idea *how* human beings flattened the dog and disappeared all the blood and innards' or *how* they kept the animals quiet, or, most importantly, *why* in the hell people would do that. She couldn't see it for what it was. Her mind was fighting her. I couldn't really blame the ranch on our fights that allowed Joyce to launch into her *I told you so* argument which validated her intuition not to buy the ranch. The invisible force had painted me into a corner with my wife.

It would be easy for anyone to ask at this point why the ranch was not sold. Money's not everything in life. Even if I lost forty percent of my initial investment, it still would have been enough to restore the peace in our lives and move forward. To this day I can't offer any reasonable answer as to why I didn't do that. It's almost as though staying there was part of the spell the place had on me. I wasn't going to let it win. At a psychological level I had been locked into some kind of ankle trap, the way old fur gatherers used to trap animals in the bush in Canada. I could not get out of the place. I could not live with myself. I could not live with the idea of giving up. The mystery of what was going on began to take root in my mind as a great mystery that I felt ordained to solve.

A Call to Arms

I started buying more weapons. I had never been a gun person, but I thought that a revolver was suitable self-defense for living in such a remote area, as I've already articulated in this story, but now I was buying more guns. I was buying long arms and automatic weapons like AK-47s. I was becoming like one of those survival nuts. I couldn't get enough weapons. I practiced a lot. The sound of machine gun fire echoed through Rainbow Valley. I put targets up and practiced my pistol, sniper rifles, and automatic weapons. I was also buying large knives and laying baseball bats and other defense items throughout the house so that there was easy access to self defense in almost any ten square feet in the house. It sounds like some cheesy action movie from Hollywood, but that's what I had been reduced to — some kind of dumb animal, cornered and beyond non-violent resolution.

Joyce made her final appeal by asking me why I would not just sell the ranch. I said it was because it was one of the largest things I'd ever taken on in my life, and I wasn't going to run away from it. That's not how I operate. What comes at me in my life I face, and

I always win. It may take a while, but I always win. We began to move away, and I told her if she needed to leave, end the marriage, or whatever she needed to do, that she needed to go do it, because I was not leaving the ranch until I was damn good and ready, and I would not leave until I got the upper hand. I didn't give a rat's ass about otherworldly or supernatural adversaries. A line had been drawn in the sand. Anything that crossed it had to deal with me.

Agreement to Stay

It was decided that we would stay at the ranch. Maybe I was a little obstinate in my position, but there is no way I was running from the ranch. Once Joyce understood my position, we stopped arguing about it. In my trips out and about in the local area during the day, when I would pack a couple of the dogs in the truck and go to town, or go to other towns, or my local feed store, or wherever, I started dropping little hints about what happened to my dog at the ranch. I learned that animal mutilations were somewhat common where I lived. People would give me a funny glance at first, then they would lean in and whisper something like, *that goes on around here.* Nobody wanted to sit down and have a coffee and talk about it at length. It was like a dirty little secret among all the people in the area, and later I found out through my research it wasn't just my area of Arizona; it was all of Arizona.

I decided to bring the local authorities into my research. I contacted the Department of Agriculture for Arizona and spoke to them. I was given an unofficial conversation with a person who worked inside the office. I was told that there would be no official confirmation of the bloodless mutilations that had been happening to Arizona ranchers for an indeterminate amount of time. The government had no official position on the phenomenon. However, off the record, the civil servant was more than happy to give me thirty minutes of his time. Yes, it was quite common for horses, cattle, sheep, and dogs to be found bloodlessly mutilated. I was told that the prevailing thesis was that it was a non-human presence that was mutilating the animals. It was an interesting choice of words, non-human. It wouldn't have been any great leap to say extraterrestrial.

In the years that I've been researching what happens to me and my wife on my ranch, I've found a tight-lipped government at every turn. There is something about the extraterrestrial phenomenon on this planet that the government just does not want to talk about. It doesn't matter how overwhelming the evidence is, how many people are having direct experiences with these bloodless mutilations and laser precise incisions into animals that surely are not the work of random poachers or vandals, the government doesn't want to talk about it.

The Maricopa County Sheriff's Office was equally tight-lipped. They gave me far less time than the Department of Agriculture. I came across a documentary called *A Strange Harvest* by Linda Moulton Howe, a reporter out of Denver Colorado who had been tracking the animal mutilation phenomenon. It was interesting to hear her say that UFOs had a part in the mutilations. Many of the farmers reported seeing orange lights in the sky and crafts just around the time of the mutilations. I couldn't believe what I was reading. It was exactly what I was experiencing at Stardust Ranch, including the orange lights in the desert. Linda has gone on to be an important figure in the exopolitics world, lecturing all around the globe on many facets of the extraterrestrial presence on the planet, but she started out as a regular television reporter drawn into the animal mutilations.

Doppelgangers

This next part of my story I tell with some trepidation, wondering if anyone will even believe it. I guess the best way to tell you is to give you an example. It started on a Friday night. Joyce and I had decided to go out for dinner in Phoenix. We were getting ready, which took a lot less time for me than it did for Joyce, and when I was dressed and ready to go, I sat and waited for Joyce in the living room. As many a man has experienced, going out in public with your woman can entail some preparation for the woman. I turned on the TV and settled in for an indeterminate period of time, knowing as all men do that to rush the situation would not do me any good whatsoever.

I was watching the news when I heard her voice behind me say, I'm ready. I turned around and there she was in a beautiful red dress, her makeup done and her lipstick on and her earrings and all of the adornments that go along with a woman presenting herself to the public alongside her man. It was a lot for a Tex-Mex restaurant in Phoenix, but who am I to change the way things have been done on this planet for millennia. Joyce went out the front door and got into the Jeep. I went out the back door and did one final reconnaissance of the animals to make sure everything was all right. The dogs were in their crates and the horses were happily docile on their range, and everything looked good, so I walked around the side of the house and up to the laneway and got into the driver's seat with Joyce who was waiting for me in the passenger seat.

I turned on the car and drove out the long dirt laneway. There was very little traffic on the highway. It was a perfect time for driving. Joyce was always more animated when we were outside of the house. In this time alone outside the house, driving with Joyce, I always met my wife again. I know that sounds strange, but she disappeared inside that house. She didn't show up too much. We'd only been married about seven years at that point, and already it seemed like the marriage was in trouble. She was a good and loyal woman and had no intention of leaving me by divorce, but being out of the house and being distant all the time was her way of surviving what was going on around us. She understood my position that to try and sell the ranch at that point would necessitate a huge loss, and she accepted that my position was to triumph over this situation.

I enjoyed hearing about her work at the FBI when we were alone and outside of the house. I knew it always made her feel good and it was something that she could talk about. I wasn't given names or actual details, because that would be a breach of her oath of office, but I was given highlights of what the crime situation in Arizona was like, and especially Phoenix.

There's organized crime all over America and every state has its variation of it. Arizona had a serious child trafficking problem and a human trafficking problem with Latin Americans that came over the border. Sheriff Joe Arpaio of Maricopa County was quite amusing and a topic that came up at the FBI quite a bit. He was like a character out of an old John Wayne movie and the federal agents found him extremely amusing and antiquated. Joe is well-liked at a federal level and got all around the country and a lot of people knew him. So the feds were cautious about stepping on his toes. Also, America is in some way still a feudal country and the title of sheriff is — within its jurisdiction — just about the most powerful person in law enforcement, so the FBI didn't bother Joe in any way.

I took my turn at small talk and explained to Joyce a new water system I had been thinking about based off of a large standing tank to better water the horses. I also explained that we needed more fencing in the back of the property, and that I was going to go to the hardware store on Monday and get the supplies. We talked about getting more dogs, I wanted to get up to twenty-six or thirty, and Joyce was fine with that. She knew I loved animals, and she wanted to be supportive. Like I said, this time alone outside the house was the only time we had an opportunity to be a married couple. The topic of the ranch and what was happening to us with the lights in the sky, the mutilated animals, and everything else, was not something we talked about in our private time outside the house. After a casual forty-five minute drive, we arrived at our destination, a Tex-Mex restaurant with a good reputation in Phoenix. I dropped Joyce off at the front door and went to park. By the time I got to the hostess stand Joyce was seated. The hostess pointed out where she had sat Joyce. I thanked her kindly and walked back to sit with my wife.

Joyce was looking at a menu. I sat down across from her at a four-person square table and picked up my menu. I made an appetizer suggestion and Joyce agreed. Our server came by and I told the delightful young lady that we would like some chips and salsa and two margaritas. She smiled in that vivacious way that servers working in a bubbly environment do and said, I'll be right back with that for you. She spun around and disappeared. While I was looking at the entrees Joyce said she was going to the ladies' room. I nodded my head without looking up and she left.

My cell phone was clipped to my belt. It was a little uncomfortable, pinching my skin, so I took it off and placed it on the table in front of me. I realized it was turned off. It was Friday night at seven 7:45 PM. I couldn't imagine anybody desperate to reach me, but I turned it on nonetheless. What's the point of having a cell phone if it's not turned on? It immediately started to beep. I had messages and missed calls. I flipped open the analog phone and saw four missed messages, all from our home number. I felt my heart sink. There was nobody at home. Was even our peace outside of the house now going to be shattered by the strange phenomenon happening at the ranch? I dialed into the voice messaging and waited to hear the first message. To my shock and disbelief, it was Joyce. She was furious — Where are you? How could you leave the house without me? Are you that insensitive and rude that you couldn't even wait for me? — I couldn't believe what I was hearing. If my wife was at home, waiting in the house, and I left without her, who in the hell just went to the bathroom?

I glanced to the back of the restaurant, the entrance hall to the washrooms. Joyce was not returning yet. I quickly dialed the home number. Joyce picked up. Where are you? she asked. I told her I was at the restaurant in Phoenix. I listened to five or seven seconds of an emotional tirade from a frustrated and exasperated wife at the end of her patience. I didn't know what to say. I was stunned. I told her that there were factors involved that I couldn't explain right at that moment but that she had to trust me. I told her I'd be home in forty-five minutes. She said okay. I hung up the phone and nervously waited for whatever it was that would come back from the washroom.

Three minutes later. I saw *Joyce* appear at the back of the restaurant, near the bathrooms. She walked back to the table and sat down. Whatever was sitting across from me was able to intuit my mood and my thoughts perfectly. I realized at that moment that I had never looked face to face with whatever I had brought to the restaurant in the entire drive to Phoenix. I had been looking out the windshield, concentrating on the road, and what I had thought was my wife looked straight ahead as well. Our conversation had taken place without looking at each other in the eyes. I dropped her off at the restaurant door and parked the car. This was the first time since I checked the animals and walked up the side of the house that I look directly into its face. The look on my face must have told whatever that thing was that I knew it was not Joyce. The eyes went completely black. I don't just mean the pupil and the iris, I mean its entire eyes turned black. I pushed my chair back and walked out of the restaurant as quickly as I could. I didn't even leave money on the table. I went out to the parking lot, got into the Jeep, backed it up, and sped off back home.

When I got home, Joyce was in the living room watching television. Her eyes and face were wet and puffy from crying. I didn't know how to tell her this new development. How do you tell someone what happened to me in the restaurant? It's beyond all reason. I don't think I've ever read anything like it anywhere, not even an HP Lovecraft novel. Somehow, the forces inside our house and around our ranch had fabricated a facsimile of my wife that was sufficient enough to fool me before I looked directly into its eyes. I drove forty-five minutes to

Phoenix with it and carried on a conversation with it as though it was my wife. In the end I did the only thing a responsible husband could do, I told Joyce the truth. While I was happy to be an honest husband and tell her the truth, I was not happy to add another layer of misery, despair, confusion, and paranormal activity at the ranch. My wife was at her breaking point already.

The doppelganger phenomenon would repeat itself several times over the years. It was always very convincing, and it always took a little bit of time for either myself or Joyce to figure out what we were dealing with was a doppelganger, and yes, it happened to Joyce as well. A second of me was created on several occasions and fooled my wife for short periods. Of all of the things that have happened at the ranch over the years, the doppelganger is among the strangest.

Part III

The Weird World of Exopolitics

Chapter 6

Engagement

Men have been biologically hardwired to defend a home since the beginning of time. In most instances the defenses are against an encroaching army or some form of invader force from another country or region or tribe; the variation in my story is that the encroachment was from some other dimension or world or solar system, a strange mix of the paranormal and the extraterrestrial. The things moving around the house were definitely what most people would associate with paranormal activity, a poltergeist, or something in that class of being. What was done to my Rottweiler, Gunner, was more in line with the extraterrestrial phenomenon, as my research had told me.

By this time in my story, Joyce and I had been on the ranch about seven years. I would like to say that we had acclimatized to the phenomenon going on around us, but that would be a bit of an exaggeration. Most of the time, we tried to pretend it wasn't happening until it got really out of hand. I continued to see the lights in the sky when I drove out into the desert in the Jeep. Things continued to disappear around the house.

A new twist emerged. Sometimes I would misplace my car keys or my wedding ring, and, while I would be walking through the house looking for the misplaced item, it would drop out of the air above me and fall on my head, then slide down my back or front and land on the floor in front of or behind me. Something was taking the things. Something in the house could make physical items disappear and materialize at a different time. Whatever was there didn't want us there. The history of the house and the bizarre reputation it had garnered among the locals, and especially among the phone installers, now made complete sense to me. I would not have wanted to come out to the ranch and install phone lines if I worked for the phone company.

What concerned me most at that time were the nocturnal activities, the scars, bruising, indentations, and branding that would appear on our bodies in the morning, not always, but always present and always recurring right around the time we would forget about it, there to remind us in the mornings when we woke up that we were living with something extremely negative and supernatural.

I became increasingly militant. I kept guns at different locations throughout the house. I had to be careful. There was a lot of brick in the interior and for those of you who are familiar with firearms, you know that brick is a difficult wall surface. Bullets tend to ricochet off brick and you could end up shooting yourself or somebody you didn't intend to shoot.

Joyce didn't question what I was doing. She understood completely. I was just being the man of the house. We were dealing with a violent presence that meant us harm. It was natural in her mind for the man of the house to go out and get arms. It was no time for any debate on firearms in the house. We were both way past that. There were knives and baseball bats and pipes in various parts of the house. Preeminent in my mind was what was done to my animals, the flattened Rottweiler and the eviscerated horses.

Another aspect of what we were going through was the extreme isolation. Things that are not of this world tend to isolate people. If you have problems with mounting debt due to a gambling problem, at some point you're just going to break down and call your brother or your brother-in-law or your parents, if they're still alive, come clean, promise to join Gamblers Anonymous, and look for a solution to the problem. Same thing with drinking, although with drinking or drugs it's usually the significant other that reaches out for help and forms an intervention.

As you go down the list of problems that human beings face, there's a solution to almost everything. All of those rules go out the window when you're dealing with something not of this world. You can't call up family and explain what was going on at our ranch. Most of my family was dead by the time I bought the ranch anyways. A series of illnesses and accidents wiped out almost all of my family in the early nineties. Joyce's family lived in Wisconsin, and they were strict

Catholics. We were not going to bother them with this stuff. They probably wouldn't believe us anyways.

You go through your list of friends. There are people that you kept in contact with from high school, maybe University, and your work friends and colleagues, social couples that you've met through your wife, things like this, and when you get to the end of this list you realize there's no one that you would call up and say hey can we go and have a coffee? I have some things to discuss with you.

I don't know what it is about this material that isolates you so much. There's a tremendous fear in all of us about talking about things which are not part of the general consensus of accepted phenomenon in this human existence. All of us deep down are very worried about being called crazy, even if we know we're telling the truth, even if we have support in the form of a husband or wife, as was the case with Joyce and I, even with all of that you don't want to go out into the public and talk about these things.

Human beings are social animals, and most of our problems are solved in the circles we socialize, family and friends. Now there are definitely things that people keep to themselves but still seek help with outside of social circles. I bare witness to this. I was a social work counselor for years. I did my graduate work at Arizona State. I worked in institutions for years. I ran a private practice. I am well familiar with all of the things that people go and see a therapist for that they would not share with their family or friends.

Everybody needs somewhere to go to let something out of them that's eating them alive. Everyone needs to check their sanity from time to time and speak to a professional. No harm no foul, and certainly no shame. For some people the therapist is substituted with a priest or rabbi, but it's the same net effect. You have someone to go and talk to about a deeply personal problem. The extremely crippling and debilitating thing about what was going on at the ranch was how much it isolated Joyce and I. We only had each other, and a lot of the time we were at each other's throats and fighting. On top of this, we are going through this living hell at the ranch.

With each passing month, and with the passing of the first year, and well into our second year at the ranch, it was as though whatever was there was becoming more and more belligerent, more daring in revealing itself. I sometimes thought that this was because it realized we were isolated. The stuff in the first year that has already been described in this book seems to me to have been designed to get us to leave the ranch. It had already crossed my mind, at this point in my sojourn at the ranch, that the poor seventeen-year-old Mexican boy was taken out, driven to suicide by the dark forces that had been working on my mind, an adult mind with psychiatric training, and even I was almost brought to my wit's end. I could only imagine what that poor boy went through.

So when assuming the role of the protector, I not only had to arm myself and be prepared for anything in the house, I also had to figure out what was going on. This took me into deep research about the history of the area and the phenomenon we were dealing with at the ranch. This is how I came into contact with all the other researchers, like Linda Moulton Howe. In the literature I came across, including the Walton abduction close to the ranch in 1976, perhaps one of the most famous abduction stories of all time, there had never been any stories about human beings killed.

The mutilations were usually livestock. They never took place too close to a ranch, but rather in the fields, when the animals were alone at night. Like my story there was never any warning, any cry of pain, or any distress at night that disturbed the animal population. If you keep dogs at a farm, you know they are extremely sensitive to everything going on around, and their chief utility is to act as an alarm system. In all of the animal mutilation stories I have come across, as I began to pour through the literature, there was never any warning given to the people.

It was the same story over and over again. They would wake up in the morning, go out to do their chores and, in the process of checking on the livestock, they would find an animal mutilated. They were not always mutilated the same way. Sometimes the sexual organs were taken. Other times the anus was bored out. In some instances, the animals were completely eviscerated. I didn't come across too many stories that resembled what happened to my Rottweiler, which was completely unbelievable. But all of the mutilations had this one thing in common: they could not have been done by any kind of livestock vandals or livestock looters.

The history of the desecration of the animals bodies was beyond even the medical practices of most hospitals. The idea of people with that kind of medical expertise sneaking around the entire country of the United States and doing this to animals was preposterous, and, of course, I must add here that the animal mutilation phenomenon was international.

Because the markings on our bodies happened at night, I became especially defensive about the bedroom. We were being attacked where we slept. Neither Joyce nor I had awoken during any of these assaults. I placed a baseball bat behind the headboard of the bed in our master bedroom. I didn't keep a gun close to the the bed, nor a knife. I didn't want to wake up half asleep and do something stupid. So a baseball bat seemed like the best form of defense in the bedroom.

I finally had an experience with the night time visitors. It was in the middle of the night. At the location of our ranch in Rainbow Valley, there wasn't a sound to be heard in the middle of the night. Back then, there weren't enough houses around for traffic much past 11:00 PM. Whatever was visiting us in the middle of the night, leaving marks and brands and indents on Joyce and I, made little or no sound, at least nothing that either one of us had heard up until that point, and certainly not enough to wake us up.

On the night of my first engagement with them, it was not a sound that brought me out of my sleep. It was touch. I had been lying in the bed for about ninety minutes with my eyes closed, unable to fall asleep. in some kind of dreamscape, in and out of consciousness, and I felt a cold and clammy *thing* touch my arm around the wrist and stroke my forearm along the inside right up to the elbow. I immediately sprang into action. I grabbed the baseball bat from behind the headboard, and I swung as hard as I could right in front of me on my side of the bed. I heard a hiss. It's a little hard to describe. The closest thing I can compare it to is if you were to take a knife and puncture a soccer ball or football. It was that sound of the sudden evacuation of air under pressure. I flipped on the night light and there they were — three of the gray aliens right inside the bedroom on my side of the bed.

They stood about four feet tall. They had no genitalia. Their arms and legs were very thin. They were a little thicker up in the chest area, and their wastes were uncommonly thin. They had large, globe-like heads with bulbous black eyes. The eyes were what haunted me the most, like insect eyes, giant fly eyes. Before I could get another hit in with the baseball bat, they literally phased out. Now I know I sound crazy, but believe me when I tell you, Joyce has seen this over the years. People who have stayed at the ranch have seen this. They literally phase out as though they're behind an invisible stage curtain.

And that was my first encounter with *the grays*.

Phoenix Lights

In each instance, each escalation of supernatural occurrence, our minds denied what was happening. Even after the doppelgangers, the mutilated animals, and lights in the sky, I fought the idea in my own mind that I brained an alien with a baseball bat. This is what trauma does. It effects our thinking. We try to change our reality. We let that old comfortable voice come back and raise doubt — Did that really happen? Maybe I dreamed it? My mind was no different. Nor is the public mind. This might be part of the reason we lie to ourselves in general.

In 1997 Phoenix experienced what has famously come to be known as the *Phoenix Lights*. Thousands of people saw the lights. In typical form, the media and government gave a horseshit cover-up story — the lights were flares dropped from a high flying bomber over the Barry Goldwater Air Range.

KTAR News recently did a memorial story on MARCH 13, 2019. The headline read:

> More than 20 years later, mystery of Phoenix Lights still fascinates people

I don't know if it's the government's desire to appear ironic, but Goldwater himself was one of the strongest proponents of full government disclosure on Arizona's extraterrestrial and UFO phenomenon. That his name would be used in a cover-up posthumously must cause him some humor wherever he is now.

> PHOENIX — Wednesday marks the 22nd anniversary of one of the strangest things to ever happen in Arizona, the Phoenix Lights phenomenon.

> Those who witnessed the bizarre lights described them as "otherworldly" and the phenomena is remembered fondly each year since it — whatever it was — was spotted.

> According to the Mutual UFO Network, on March 13, 1997 between 7:30 and 10:30 p.m., thousands of people reported seeing strange, bright lights flying over Nevada, Arizona and part of Mexico.

"It wasn't just one event, there were many events across the state for more than 12 hours," Phoenix Lights Network spokeswoman Lynne Kitei said.

The first event was described as a V-shaped object the size of a commercial plane soaring through the sky.

Eyewitness reports thoroughly debunk the government's flare cover story.

One witness from Prescott who wished to be known only as J.R. said he watched a boomerang-shaped object glide over Granite Mountain, and it was at least a mile wide. He said there's no way it was from this planet.

"We don't have anything that big," he said. "It was totally silent. I've never seen anything even close to the colors from the exhaust that propelled that thing. It was as big as downtown Prescott and completely blocked out the stars."

Another witness was a police officer.

The second event was reported by an unidentified former Arizona police officer who claimed he saw a series of stationary, orange and red lights hanging over the Valley.

The Governor hit a new high note for government mockery.

The Phoenix Lights were treated as a joke at first by then-Gov. Fife Symington, who had an aide dress as an alien for a press conference about the phenomenon.

"This just goes to show that you guys are entirely too serious," Symington said then.

However, Symington later did a complete 180 and not only said he saw the lights himself, but believed them to be of otherworldly origin.

"I'm a pilot, and I know just about every machine that flies," Symington said. "It was bigger than anything that I've ever seen. It remains a great mystery. Other people saw it, responsible people. I don't know why people would ridicule it."

There was no denying it, though, I was living in a UFO state, and my ranch was a place of high activity.

What worried me about the grays in the bedroom, who clearly where the parties responsible for leaving the marks on my body and Joyce's body, was the specter of abduction. This marked a new field of inquiry and research for me. I dove in to it head first. Of course, there had already been movies made about this phenomenon, and there was all kinds of literature out there, but reading about it and experiencing it are two completely different things. I now had to contend with the idea that I was being abducted, and that my wife was being abducted. Much of the literature speaks about not remembering abductions.

It became painfully clear to me that the marks on our bodies were the result of things done to us when we were abducted. And as I said, there was nobody to talk to about this. It left me very alone. I felt impotent, powerless, and vulnerable. Maybe that's why I was over-compensating with all the weapons. All of the weapons on earth are designed to kill human beings. I wasn't even sure at that point whether these creatures could be killed. I brained one with a baseball bat and all it did was hiss. It didn't matter, though. I didn't have any other options. I would fight this fight the only way I knew how to fight. Even if it was completely futile. I cannot begin to express to you the sense of violation. It felt like getting raped.

Chapter 7

The Mormon Tax Man and Desert Shoes

The direct encounter with the grays at night time was more than a little bit disturbing. Put yourself in my shoes. Human beings are built for experiences far outside what any reasonable person might call normal. You would be amazed at what a human being can assimilate. Normal is a place people gather to pretend we live in a world we understand. Normal is a bus stop on planet earth in the middle of a nearly infinite multiverse, full of dimensions separated by frequency. Human ears can only hear sounds within a certain sound range. That total sound range represents maybe less than one percent of all of the vibrations that would constitute a sound. And yet within that one percent we have an entire reality to live within. The same goes for our sight. Our eyes are created to see things within a certain light spectrum, which represents about one percent of the total light spectrum, yet we have an entire reality built around what we can see and hear on planet earth.

My normal had been blown wide open, leaving me naked and vulnerable in a new reality I had no experience with. I had heard of the gray aliens before. It was hard not to, especially with the *X-Files* on TV. They were the race of aliens that everybody associated with the abductions. They were said to be extremely unpleasant and frightening. I can't say the nighttime encounter was pleasant, but, at the same time, I wasn't chilled to my bone the way most people might be. I have a different sort of constitution. It takes a lot to cause me distress. Miraculously, Joyce didn't wake up. People who snore heavy sleep heavy. Nonetheless, I told her the next morning. It was something of a relief for her. Just as it was something of a relief for me. I think all people want mystery to end. And for us, the mystery of what was in the house had ended. It was not the sum total of what was in our house, but I don't want to get ahead of my story.

The gray took a baseball bat to the head, and the little bastard didn't go down. I was going to have to up my game. I think part of their modus operandi is to stay hidden. Once they're known, the visitations become much more frequent. Maybe they had always been frequent and I had never woken up before. God knows what they were doing in the bedroom. But now that I knew about them they were far less subtle in their coming and going. I started to see them on the ranch quite frequently. In the daytime, the evening, the dawn when I was up, and in the middle of the night when they woke me.

My encounters escalated to gunfire. Bullets didn't kill them. They made their hissing sound when they got shot, like a soccer ball being stabbed, a soft expulsion of air, but they didn't fall to the ground like human beings. We human beings can normalize a lot of things, but waking up in the middle of the night for a gunfight with gray aliens is not one of the things that's on that list. I didn't know for sure if they were coming for me or Joyce or both of us. But we started sleeping in different bedrooms.

It didn't help. They managed to find us no matter where we went. It wasn't an every night occurrence. It's hard to describe the frequency. The time between visits was long enough you could forget the visitations were going on. It was a little bit like having vermin in your house. Every once in a while you'd see the mouse but not all the time. I quickly gave up on the guns. If they didn't stop the grays, there was no point in using them. They're too dangerous. I had to think of a new way to deal with them.

As all of this was going on, I had to deal with the more perfunctory aspects of running a ranch. I needed somebody to do my taxes, and so I began to look for a reputable accountant. A gentleman in the area was recommended to me, and I went to visit him. He was the head of the Mormon Church. In their church structure the head of a certain region or jurisdiction is the bishop. He ran an office out of a strip mall in Buckeye. I didn't make an appointment. I just walked in one day. He was an affable fellow as most Mormons are, then again, they are a conversion religion, so they always have a sales mandate when they're meeting with you. I know a little bit about their doctrine, and, oddly enough, it's an extraterrestrial doctrine. Mormons believe in a universe with multiple planets inhabited by human life.

I can't remember how long after the open encounters with the grays this meeting with the Mormon accountant was. Time has sort of blurred for me now over the two decades plus that I've lived here at the ranch. I'm doing my best to give you some kind of a chronology in this story, but please forgive me if I can't get everything down to the day and month. If you study your own history, you'll notice that it's event-driven, not date driven. That's the way the human mind works. Our memory centers around events that have great emotional value, whether that value is extreme suffering or extreme joy. Most of my experience at the ranch has been trauma, which is a very defined event marker in human memory.

For the purposes of this story, we will refer to the Mormon Bishop as Fred. On my first visit to his strip mall office I was offered a water, which I accepted. I sat down in a chair in front of his desk. He asked what he could do for me. I told him I needed an accountant to manage the taxes for a new business which I had undertaken. He asked about the business. I explained to him it was a ranch, and that I was going to be offering an animal shelter for abandoned dogs and horses, and that I wanted to operate as a non-profit. He seemed quite pleased with the idea. He began to detail some of the problems with non-profits and some of the unique aspects of the accounting, and then he got around to location. When I told him where my ranch was the blood went out of his face.

That place has quite a reputation, he said.

I assured him I knew nothing of the reputation before I bought it, and that I felt in a lot of ways I had been taken advantage of by the Realtor. That's why I didn't sell. I gave him my stock answer, the same answer I've given everybody for two and a half decades. I'm not going to be run off my property by anything.

He asked me what was going on at the ranch. I gave him the briefest overview without telling him about the gray aliens. I told him about things disappearing and dropping out of the air on top of my head. I told him about the fridge door opening and food flying out of the fridge, and I told him about pots and pans rattling around in the kitchen. Maybe I should have told him about the gray aliens. I don't know. Put yourself in my position. How many people would you tell? The funny thing about public opinion about something, and the *X-Files* had given everybody a public opinion, is that you can't get any clean and objective interpretation of phenomenon.

I have sometimes thought over the years that the world of fiction is a precursor, a kind of avant-garde for human consciousness and what it's going to be dealing with in reality. The *X-Files* was a perfect example of this. The problem is, once the idea is out in the open through fiction, anyone who comes across the idea in real life immediately assumes that you're imitating the drama from a television show like the *X-Files* to garner attention for yourself. It's really quite astounding how simple and primitive the human mind is. So I left the aliens out when I described the ranch to Fred the Mormon accountant.

After coming up with a tax strategy and a pricing plan, Fred got back to the ranch. I guess he wanted to do me some kind of a solid. Maybe it was an attempt to get me into the Mormon Church. Who can say? But he straight-up asked me, Have you ever thought about an exorcism?

I told him no, I had never thought about getting the ranch exorcised.

It was then that I began to regret not talking about the aliens. His mind had set on a spiritual disturbance on the ranch. Everyone in Buckeye knew the history of my ranch. They knew about the brothel, and they knew about the shootout with the white supremacy group, the Sons of Gestapo, and they knew about the teenage boy putting the shotgun in his mouth the day of his high school graduation. It was not hard to understand why the bishop thought the place might be haunted. I had gotten myself into a jackpot there. Fred wasn't going to take no for an answer. We set a date for an exorcism about a month in the future. He said he needed some time to prepare, to confer with his congregation, and to decide which of his congregants were ready and capable of assisting him in the spiritual cleansing of my ranch.

I continued some of my daytime activities when Joyce was at work. I tinkered around the ranch — installed new water systems, repaired fences, tended to the animals, went to the feed store, and spent time with the dogs, two at a time — I also continued to go out into the desert in the Jeep. I began to enjoy this more and more. There's something quite peaceful about the desert. It's very barren, flat, loaded with scrub brush, and full of different kinds of engaging colors from red and orange to a kind of coffee colored earth, based on the iron content. The rising rock formations, the mountains in the distance, and the way the sky sat on top of the whole desert calmed me somehow.

Joyce was not thrilled about the Mormons. She felt ashamed. I could understand where she was coming from. A lot of times when you have really negative activity going on, your knee-jerk reaction is to think that people are going to blame you, somehow think that you're responsible for what's going on around you, that you're what's attracting the evil, and that you're going to be judged as such. I assured her to the best of my ability that the Mormon Bishop understood the history of the ranch and made no such designation and placed no judgment upon us for the negative activity going on at the ranch. In a moment of conversational victory over me, she smugly asked if I told him about the gray aliens. I said I had not. She smiled and made eye contact with me until it was so uncomfortable I had to look away. We both understood. There are some things we were both embarrassed about and would not talk about in public, reinforcing her position about the exorcism. She was worried about Mormons coming into the house. If they had any success in cleaning up the house, would there be an obligation on us to join the Mormon Church, which Joyce had no interest in doing whatsoever, and, truth be told, neither did I. Anyway, it was decided, the Mormon Bishop and a couple of his congregants would come over and say some prayers, walk around the house with their holy instruments, and make themselves feel good. If it had any effect on what was going on at the ranch, that would just be an ancillary benefit to Joyce and I, but we both felt a little bit guilty about not talking about the alien presence.

The appointed day finally came for the Mormon bishop and his congregants to arrive. I got the phone call that they were fifteen minutes out, so I went out and opened up the front gate and then walked back to the house and waited for them. A minivan turned into my long laneway a little while later, and I watched it slowly amble up the laneway. The bishop was in the front passenger seat. The driver was unknown to me. The side door slid open, revealing one other person in the minivan, for a total of three. They wore white shirts and dark slacks with patent leather shoes, and they were all clean cut and looked like Mormons. I opened the front door as they walked up. I greeted them all. Joyce was there with me and she greeted them all as well. They had a solemnity about them, an aura of their mission. They each in their own way looked a little bit disturbed and a little bit confused. We offered refreshments like water and cake but they wanted to get right down to business. The bishop had a small black satchel with him. He went over to a side table, placed it down, and opened it up. He handed a string of beads to each of them, and he placed a string of beads around his own neck. He pulled out a Bible and then closed the satchel. They turned to face one another and leaned their heads in like a football huddle. I couldn't hear what was being said. The bishop spoke in a low voice. The acolytes were younger than him. I would place them in their late twenties or early thirties. I imagined they were being groomed to become Mormon exorcists themselves. My ranch was a testing ground for them. When they broke their huddle, the bishop turned and looked at Joyce and I. He made deliberate eye contact with each of us and held it for several seconds. He bowed his head and then turned to begin.

The bishop led the way, holding the Bible in front of him, his two acolytes walking behind him, the three of them forming a kind of triangle, the way geese fly south in the winter. They were all reciting prayers, their lips moving and soft humming Whispers coming out of them. They intermittently closed and opened their eyes, as if they were trying to maintain a connection to their inner selves and the outer reality they had to negotiate.

Joyce and I stood off to the side and watched them. It didn't take long for the house to have a reaction. I don't know how to describe the sound we heard. From an engineering point of view, it was coming from the water pipes. It sounded like something was trying to create a voice out of the pipes. It sounded like a moan, a grumble, a lamentation. There's no physical way that water pipes could have made that sound. The bishop and his acolytes did not change their behavior one bit. They continued to walk through the house slowly and deliberately, reciting their prayers. The sound grew louder. It moved around the house. They entered each room they passed, standing inside the room for a brief time reciting prayers. When they came to the master bedroom, one of the acolytes became extremely distressed. The bishop broke his concentration to address the young man. Joyce and I could not hear what was said, but presumed it was some form of confidence-boosting, some form of feet to the fire, strength to the task, faith in the lord approach to the situation. And then, just like that, the situation turned. The hunter suddenly became the hunted. The acolytes and the bishop had looks of extreme distress on their faces. The acolyte who first showed weakness bent over and vomited. He started to turn a kind of green. It was like he got botulism in thirty seconds. The bishop was consumed with tending to him and gave up the task of reciting his prayers. There was a banging in the walls. The whole house had a malevolent feel. Joyce and I stood in the center of the living room sort of bemused by the whole situation.

As the Mormon exorcism team began to fall apart, the sound grew louder and moved through the house. The bishop gave a signal to his two acolytes for everybody to leave the house. They made a hasty retreat out the side door. Whatever they stirred up followed them outside and the one who got sick continued to vomit, then, with a slight respite from the upheavals of his stomach, he ran to the minivan and locked himself inside. The bishop and his one remaining support person tried to continue on with the prayers as the sound went down the well and echoed from the bottom like a growling and snarling demonic beast. That was about the limit of the bishop's tolerance. He grabbed his one remaining acolyte, hightailed it to the car, got in, pulled out quickly and drove away.

Joyce and I stood outside for a couple minutes, speechless and dumbfounded. Then I looked at her and said, You think that was aliens?

She turned and looked me in the eyes and just shook her head, No.

The one thing that the Mormon visit did point out was that there was more going on at the ranch than just aliens. It seems as though I was living in some kind of lower fourth dimension bus station, replete with disembodied spirits, perhaps some demonic presence, and whatever else we had not yet encountered. The one thing I firmly understood after the encounter with the Mormons was that the ranch was a unique place on the planet.

Chapter 8

The Levitating Wife

I feel like saying, *now the story gets weird*, but if you have stayed with me this long, it might be a bit of an understatement. How much weirder could it get? Wait for it.

Because I had trained myself to sleep rather lightly, always on the watch for gray aliens in the bedroom, I became aware of the fact that my wife, Joyce, was sometimes levitating in the middle of the night. Always half sleep, I had trained myself to open my eyes at the slightest disturbance. Sometimes I would open my eyes for no reason at all. It was one of these times — no reason at all — that I happened to see my wife floating three feet off the mattress in the master bedroom. I thought I was dreaming at first. I thought I must be still sleeping and dreaming. I gave my head a shake. I sat straight up. No motion or sound I made seemed to disturb the trance that she was in three feet above the bed, her nightgown sort of wafting in a light breeze.

I got up on my knees and placed my mouth level with her ear. I called her name several times — Joyce, Joyce, Joyce — to no avail. She was in a state of consciousness that was deeper than sleep. I put my arms all around her body, on the top and bottom, at her feet and at her head. There were no strings or devices holding her up. I decided I had to do something drastic. I grabbed her by the shoulders and called her name very loudly — Joyce! She opened her eyes. I applied pressure downward on her shoulders, and she came back down to the bed. She looked at me as though she was dreaming. She closed her eyes and went back to sleep.

The next morning at breakfast, I put her food and coffee in front of her and I said, Sweetheart, do you remember levitating three feet off the bed last night?

An incredulous look crossed her face, No, She said.

Joyce, dear, you were levitating three feet off the bed last night, completely asleep, in a horizontal position. It was like a magic act, some David Copperfield stuff.

I broke through her in incredulity. Are you serious?

I'm afraid so, I said.

How can I levitate?

We held eye contact for about thirty seconds in silence. It was another question we couldn't answer.

It started to happen more and more. I would wake up and Joyce would be levitating above the bed. It reached a point where I would find her levitating in positions other than above the bed. Sometimes I would find her levitating and moving slowly. She was always moving toward the bedroom door. In these instances I would have to get out of bed and go and lay a hand on her ankle and stop whatever traction motion was pulling her away from the bed. One time I caught her in the middle of the hall. I woke up and she wasn't in bed, I saw no light in the bathroom off the master bedroom, so I assumed she was somewhere else in the house in the middle of the night. Curious, I got up and went to look for her. She was halfway down the hall toward the screen door, levitating and moving slowly, and when I say slowly, I mean a little bit slower even than a walking pace, perhaps the walking pace of an old lady with a walker.

In every instance, once I finally got her to open her eyes, she would slowly descend to the floor, sit up, then stand up, and calmly walk back to bed. In each of these instances she had no recollection the following morning at breakfast of what had happened. This, as you might well imagine, put a strain on our marriage. Joyce had to believe that I was telling her the truth, because she had no recollection of it. Of course, that said, with everything we had seen going on at the ranch, it wasn't a huge leap of faith for her to believe that she was levitating above the bed, outside of the bedroom, and down the hallway towards a final destination we did not know. This finally reached a dramatic conclusion one night when I was unable to wake her up even by grabbing her ankles. Nor was I able to stop the slow movement three feet off the ground, down the hallway, and out the side wall — she went right through the wall. All I could do was walk beside her to see where the traction beam was taking her. When I got outside, using the door, I looked up and there was a metallic disc in the air, maybe a hundred feet off the ground, and maybe a hundred feet in diameter, and out of it was coming a blue-white light.

I ran back into the house and got an AK-47. Joyce was moving underneath the center of the disk. The blue-white light was still fixed on her. I trained the AK-47 on the source of the light underneath the disk. I opened up with the banana clip, which, for those of you who don't know guns, is two clips taped together upside down, so that when one runs out, you pull it out quickly, turn the clips 180 degrees and reinsert into the AK-47. Whatever I did, it worked. The blue white-light disappeared and Joyce was dropped to the ground. This time she did wake up fully. This time she did have a full recall of what had happened.

Looking for Answers

My introduction to and movement into the world of exopolitics continued under the tutelage of a man named Captain Robert Collins.

His biography reads as follows on the Coast-to-Coast website, a popular syndicated national radio station which deals with fringe topics:

> Robert Collins was career Air Force serving in the fields of Avionics, Ground Communications, Engineering Physics and Intelligence (Foreign Technology Division, Wright-Pat) gaining an in-depth understanding of all the career fields. After 22 years he left public service to pursue the subject of UFOs full time living on Air Force retirement supplemented by odd jobs. In his many adventures within the Air Force he was turned onto the world of UFOs by Ernie Kellerstrass in 1985. Ernie was a retired AF Lt Col who worked at the FTD (Foreign Technology Division) until retiring. After performing some research he concluded that the government UFO cover-up was real and went to great lengths to uncover the cover-up which spanned over 60 years.

Collins was absolutely fascinated by my story at Stardust Ranch. He understood the implications right away. He was familiar with the Bradshaw Ranch and the Skinwalker Ranch, and he knew both had been largely closed off to public scrutiny and the scrutiny of independent UFO researchers like himself. He did his very best to court me and bring me into the UFO world with my unique story.

Collins introduced me to a man by the name of Peter Gersten who lived in Phoenix at the time. Gersten had made a name for himself taking the government to court through the Freedom of Information Act to force the release of documents related to UFOs. He was quite fascinated with my material as well, Gersten admonished me to make postings to his website, which at the time was called Citizens Against UFO Secrecy (CAUS), with a similarly named website.

The mission statement, still available online today, reads:

> Citizens Against UFO Secrecy (CAUS) is a nonprofit corporation which stands for two principles:
>
> 1. It is against any and all secrecy relating to contact with all forms of extraterrestrial intelligence
> 2. It believes that the public has the absolute and unconditional right to know about this contact.
>
> CAUS believes that the people on this planet are (1) being contacted, directly and indirectly, and will continue to be contacted at an ever increasing rate as we approach the galactic alignment; and (2) we presently have the technology and resources to discover the truth about this extraterrestrial contact for ourselves and decipher these messages. Pursuant to these principles, CAUS is involved to specific projects to get the truth out:
>
> 1. A Freedom of Information Act (FOIA) lawsuit to be filed against the Army based upon the book "Day After Roswell" attributed to Lt. Col. (ret) Philip Corso.
> 2. "Project:Destination Moon,' the first civilian, privately financed, rocket to the moon to send back live photos from Sinus Medii to verify alleged artificial structures located there
> 3. The CAUS INITIATIVE, a viable and practical alternative to Congressional hearings, immunity and amnesty
> 4. 'Beyond a Reasonable Doubt,' a promotional and fundraising video on behalf of CAUS.

Other projects will involve:

1. interpretation and analysis of crop circles data
2. investigation and analysis of photos, videos and films of UFOs
3. collection and analysis of channeled information.

Gersten made something of a name for himself in the UFO world when, through a Freedom of Information Act case against the Central Intelligence Agency, he managed to get some nine hundred documents released. An additional fifty-seven documents were withheld due to what the CIA called *national security*.

Like many in the UFO world, he hasn't aged well. *The Phoenix Times* had the following story in 2012. Apparently Gersten had decided that a portal was going to open in conjunction with the Mayan calendar, and, if he leaped from a tall rock, he would go through the portal and end up in another dimension.

The exopolitics world is full of people who go a little off their rocker. There's something supernatural about the whole thing. I have avoided that by just staying consistent with what I experienced and trying not to extrapolate too much. However, I do understand where Gersten was going with this. There is a connection between our religions and our spiritual beliefs and the exopolitics world.

Here's Gersten in the 2012 article from *The Phoenix Times*.

Sedona Vortex Jumper Peter Gersten [1]

Wanders Home After Vortex Fails to Open

ERIC TSETSI | DECEMBER 22, 2012 | 2:37PM

Sedona resident Peter Gersten was left high and dry last night after a vortex failed to open at the base of Bell Rock, the popular red rock hiking spot. Gersten had been planning to leap into the "portal" last night. Instead, he apparently wandered home in an anticlimactic ending to his Doomsday stunt.

"He went home," says Yavapai County Sheriff's Office spokesman Dwight D'Evelyn.

---

[1] https://www.phoenixnewtimes.com/content/printView/6648932 2/2

"His earthly home in Sedona."

Here's Gersten's original explanation of what he was doing on Bell Rock all day yesterday:

"On the Winter Solstice of 2012 at exactly 11:11 UT a cosmic portal will open in Sedona Arizona and a leap of faith - from the top of Bell Rock - will propel me through its opening," he wrote.

A couple months ago, Gersten told us in an e-mail, "I will be on the top of Bell Rock on 12-21-2012 from at least 11:00 am to either midnight or the manifestation of an extraordinary event - whichever comes first."

Gersten, a retired lawyer – who, at one point, became "professionally involved with the UFO phenomenon" – detailed his lead-up to the opening of a portal at the base of Sedona's Bell Rock for at least two years.

Here's what Gersten himself said:

Most of you will think that I am delusional and that my insane act will certainly result in my death. Death is inevitable - at least nowadays - and 100 years from now it won't matter whether I died in 2012 or 2013 or even 2020. But I believe that some type of cosmic portal will be opening at that time and place and that an opportunity will present itself. I fully expect that it will either lead to the next level of this cosmic program; freedom from an imprisoning time-loop; a magical Martian-like bubble; or something equally as exotic.

In March 2012 I will reach 70 years of age and nine months later we arrive at the cosmic coordinate. I think it will then be time for me to move on - in one form or another. I'd like to see what else our Cosmic Computer has to offer. Well, that's that. We can all get on with our holidays now.

I don't blame the media and the establishment for mocking a lot of the people in the UFO movement. They make fools of themselves. The entire way the UFO movement is brought forward is suspect from top to bottom.

Gersten encouraged me to send him stories about things that had happened or were happening on my ranch for his website. I complied. It was one of the first places in the public sphere that I began to talk about my story. It's necessary that you understand when a person is having these kinds of experiences there is a tendency to try to keep them private. They are, after all, happening to me and my wife. They are not happening to anybody else. For that reason alone they remained very personal. By this time, I really had no choice. I had to begin to talk about this in public. I had to begin to look for help with this situation.

Another person of interest in the UFO world is Clifford Stone. Like so many others he has a military background, and, like the others, he waited until retirement to begin his work of *uncovering* the truth about UFOs and delivering it to the world. Curious how that works. Here's his short biography from Gaia.[2]

> Clifford Stone has become a monumental figure in the disclosure movement. He served 22 years in the U.S. Army where he worked with an elite secret group which was dispatched to crash sites with orders to recover extraterrestrial craft, bodies and technology. He states that the recovery of these artifacts has allowed the U.S. government to make astounding advancements in science and technology which could benefit the world – if these discoveries were to be made public. He claims to have personally cataloged 57 species of alien life forms.
>
> His personal experience has made him a highly qualified expert in alien technology, black ops organizations/procedures, and the history of extraterrestrial contact.
>
> Since his retirement, Stone has become devoted to diligently searching government archives and amassing one of the largest private collections of authentic government documents pertaining UFOs and extraterrestrials. He seeks the release of the all of the evidence, information and materials

---

[2]https://www.gaia.com/video/clifford-stone-bio

which show that intelligent life has been visiting our planet, and influencing our government, for a long time.

The reason I bring Stone up at this point is that he had a unique experience in the UFO world that brings a spiritual dimension to it. Stone claims that he acted as the principal communicator with an alien that the United States Government had recovered from a crash. Stone developed a tremendous empathy for the being. He spoke about this relationship years later in interviews after retiring from the military, and he spoke very fondly of the alien. The way he spoke about the being, he seemed to raise it up to a higher order than human beings. The principal characteristic of the being was its empathy for other beings and it's love, which Stone said was much superior to an average human being. It did not want to hurt anything. Sensing Stone's sadness over a recent loss, Stone claims the being arranged a meeting between himself and his dead son.

Now ask yourself this: what kind of a physically present being could arrange a meeting between the living and the dead? The world of UFOs and extraterrestrials is not what we are discussing in public at all. It's my belief that the extraterrestrials do not travel vast distances to come to planet Earth. Instead, they use another means of movement that is beyond physical. And they travel through the worlds that we live in after we drop our physical bodies.

Imagine the implications here. Imagine the implications for the Vatican. Imagine the implications for the Mormons. Imagine the implications for virtually every religious teaching on this planet. We are told fairy tales by men who wear robes about the world we live and the world we will occupy when we die, and the extraterrestrials visiting us today may have direct experience they can share with us that redefines everything we know about life and death. The truth is, it's much closer to what Einstein said: energy never dies it just changes form.

There are entire storylines out there in the UFO world which suggests that the extraterrestrials are the angels that visited us in the past. The extraterrestrial phenomenon might be the baptism, the initiation the human race has been waiting for. According to Clifford Stone, we're still too violent and primitive to interact with the vast majority of them. The ones that are visiting us are of a lower order spiritually, demons, if you will, to round out the religious allegory.

So the question persists: what was happening at my ranch? Why would Joyce and I be waking up with marks and brands on our body? Why did the grays keep reappearing in the house? Why was my wife floating down the hall, through a wall, and out the house, to be taken up by a white-blue light into a disc? What the hell was I interacting with and what did they want from us?

To round out the trans-dimensional motif, let's entertain the idea that a human being exists on multiple dimensions at the same time, the higher dimensions being unconscious to us because of the gross energies of our sense-mind life. The way I have come to understand it is as follows. If you went to the wildest place you could find in the world, maybe Siberia, maybe the rainforest where Bruce MacDonald, my coauthor for this work, lives, you would see a perfect circle of life where no one expression of life was allowed to overpopulate because it was checked by another expression of life that consumed it.

This is the basic ecosystem they teach us in high school biology. It's always a circle. If it were not a circle the entire system would become unbalanced and would fail. That is the principle of ecology and ecosystems. Now, understand that the parts of the human being that rest unconscious at higher states of awareness on other planes of existence emit energies of a psychic nature which are consumed by other beings that do not have a physical form, or cannot take or manifest physical form without the energy they get from us. Essentially, this is the Gnostic story of the archons in the Gnostic bible, *The Nag Hammadi Library*. We are a source of food at a non-physical level for entities of a decrepit nature that are gravitating towards us because of our low vibration, our course emotions, and our generally negative nature as human beings. We are part of an ecosystem we do not yet understand.

Chapter 9

Desert Mysteries

I was driving out in the desert with two of the dogs, and I had an intuitive nudge to stop the Jeep and turn off the engine. I did. It was a little after noon, the hottest part of the day, and some days it could get up to one hundred and twenty-five degrees Fahrenheit. I grabbed a water canteen and left the Jeep with the dogs to go on a little walkabout. I didn't usually do this. Sometimes I stopped if I saw something, a metal object or something that I might want to get out of the vehicle and pick up, but, for the most part, I stayed in the Jeep with the air conditioning on. The conditions outside the Jeep in the middle of the day were just too rigorous for a human being to survive very long. There was a small hill about a hundred meters off in the distance and my intuition was guiding me towards it. With the two Rottweilers at my side I felt fairly secure. I also had a 357 handgun strapped to my hip. The water canteen was over my shoulder, and I had a good pair of walking boots and a straw cowboy hat to keep the sun off my head.

When I crested the small hill, I looked down upon a little valley in which there was a circle where all of the growth was missing. Now this was a very odd thing. There was no rational explanation for all the missing vegetation. The desert is by no means a rainforest, but what does grow there grows consistently, across every square yard of the desert. In this particular spot, a circumference of about two-hundred yards, what struck me was it had the same kind of look as a crop circle, where everything was just missing instead of the usual crop circle design. The desert floor was bald and naked of any vegetation or scrub. If that was not weird enough, in the center of this barren circle was a

81

second circle, a circle of shoes. I walked down the small hill and examined the shoes. There were hundreds of pairs. The circumference of the circle of shoes was about a hundred yards. organized into men's shoes, women's shoes, children's shoes, and a fourth group which I would describe as miscellaneous. They were all in pairs and the toes were all pointing in towards the center of the circle.

I wanted to get the camcorder in the truck. It was always in the glove compartment. The oddity of Stardust Ranch and Rainbow Valley had made me an amateur videographer. I wanted to get the circle of shoes on video. I walked back to the truck, sipping some water as I did, no rush to my movement, the dogs lazily walking beside me, the sun as intense on them as it was on me. I opened the passenger door and retrieved the camcorder. I went back to where the circle of shoes was. I trained the camera lens on the circle of shoes and hit record.

As I stood there, trying to figure out why there would be a circle of shoes in the middle of the desert, and why there would be an area of no vegetation in a perfect circle, I started to feel what I can only describe as an electrical charge. The hair on my arms stood up. Something had changed in the atmosphere. The dogs were both lying down beside me, their stomachs on the ground, their chins buried in their front legs, with a submissive position, a docile position. I turned around. What was behind me was beyond anything I'd ever fathomed before. It was a giant black triangle, a ship. It was it at least as big as a football field, maybe bigger. I could see lights underneath it. It was just hovering off the ground, about a hundred feet away from me, and about a hundred feet off the ground. It seemed to be just stopped there, looking at me. That's the last thing I remember. I went unconscious.

The camcorder kept going. The digital video shot indicated that I had been unconscious for an hour, under the blazing sun of the desert. The dogs were beside me. When I started to wake up they immediately licked my face. Their saliva was a nice balm. All three of us were extremely dehydrated. My skin had been burned to a crisp. I could feel the tightness of my face, and I could feel the skin almost wanting to jump off my arms. My legs and torso were okay because I had pants and a shirt on, albeit short-sleeved. I was groggy but managed to stand up. My balance came back to me after about ten seconds. I stopped the camcorder. It wasn't quite an hour I had been unconscious; it was fifty-five minutes. I don't know what knocked me unconscious. I stumbled back to the truck, rehydrated myself and the dogs, apologized profusely to the dogs for what I had put them through, closed all the windows in the truck, turned on the engine, and put on the air-conditioning. The camcorder had been on for fifty-five minutes but nothing had been recorded.

After about ten minutes of cooling down, I put the truck in drive and headed back home. When Joyce got home I was asleep on the sofa. My face was as red as a tomato, as were my arms. She came over and woke me up. I told her the story. She made another petition for us to leave the ranch and Rainbow Valley. I shook my head like the obstinate son-of-a-bitch that I am.

No, I said. I'm not going anywhere.

The more strange the ranch and the surrounding area became, the more entrenched I became in my position.

My fascination with the desert did not abate. I don't know if I'm just straight-up stupid or the fear gene is something I don't have, like some kind of emotional leprosy. I kept going into the desert, exploring the area around my ranch. I had one long disappearance, eighteen hours I could not account for, and I woke up far from home and naked. I had to walk barefoot through the desert under the blaring sun for hours to find my way home. This still didn't deter me from going into the desert.

Native History

Arizona is an ancient part of the United States. It is home to the Hopi Indians and the Navajo Indians, among others. I see artifacts of these cultures all through the desert in stone carvings. Adobe structures are still standing a thousand years later, and there are markings on the walls of caves and mountainsides. Very close to my ranch are the Es-trella Mountains. They were named so by the Jesuits in the eighteen hundreds. By some bizarre twist of fate, estrella means star in Span-ish, so the Jesuits named them the star mountains. Perhaps the Jesuits themselves experienced something celestial in that part of Arizona.

Archaeologists say that the history of the area goes back at least ten thousand years. Nomads entered first, hunters and gatherers, then ev-idence shows they began to settle into agriculture and permanent liv-ing. The earliest recorded people are called the Anasazi. It's a Navajo word meaning enemy ancestors. Somewhere around a thousand years ago they started building little Villages carved right into the mountain-sides. It's quite an architectural feat. The archaeological record shows a desertion of the area around the twelfth and thirteenth centuries. Nobody really knows why the Anasazi left their homes. Some postulate drought. Another group called the Sinagua, which means without water in Spanish, developed alongside the Anasazi. They may have deserted their homes as well around the same time.

By far the most prolific tribal peoples in the area are and were the Hopi. They have a huge reservation in the north of Arizona, one and a half million acres. There are eleven main Hopi villages. A group called the old are widely considered to be the oldest group of people living in the United States. As of the year 2000, the Hopi population was about seven thousand on the reserve. The Hopi are most likely the direct descendants of the Anasazi. They found their way into the new age world with some prophecies that were made some time ago and with an understanding of the stars that belies their technology, things like the complete lack of telescopes and any concept of astronomy. Nonetheless, their knowledge of the star systems is quite unique. Again, One of the many mysteries dotting the areas in Arizona. The Hopi are also known for a very deep and rich spiritual life. Most of the rituals that they perform are meant to bring in crops. They were trying to bring in corn and other things to sustain themselves in an area that gets an annual rainfall of about twelve inches. The Hopi people believe in harmony with environment.

The Navajo people came much later and it's believed they came from as far away as Alaska and Canada. Their migration took place sometime around a thousand years ago. They mirrored the agricultural lifestyle of the Hopi. The Navajo nation today encompasses about a quarter million people and just under three thousand square miles of reserve in the Four Corners area of Arizona.

Another native group is called the Yavapai. This loosely translates to sun people. They claim to be among the first people in the Sedona, Arizona region according to the Yavapai creation story. They tell a story that is remarkably similar to Noah's Ark. The lady of the pearl was put inside a log with a woodpecker and sent from Montezuma to prepare for a great flood, and flood it did. It rained for forty days and forty nights. The water receded. The log came to rest in Sedona, and the woodpecker freed the beautiful young woman and led her on a journey to the Mingus Mountain with the white stone or pearl her people had given her for protection.

And then there were the Apache. They were the descendants of people who came from the northeast sometime around the ninth century. They frequently conflicted with the pueblo people in New Mexico and their name, Apache, might come from a Zuni word for enemy. They garnered a fierce reputation as warriors in the Four Corners native population among the Spanish and the US forces that fought them during the long Indian Wars. They were a little more nomadic than the other native populations in Arizona, changing location quite often to pursue the animals they hunted for sustenance. Horses weren't introduced until the Spanish came, but the moment the Apache got a hold of them they became nearly mythic horse masters.

As I became more interested in the early history of Arizona, and specifically the desert, I would often wonder if any of these native peoples had the experiences I had. I wondered if they had been abducted, if they had met aliens, if they had seen the lights in the sky? My default answer is yes. It certainly explains the Hopi cosmology, but the Hopi cosmology means that there was a transfer of information, which suggests a peaceful and amicable extraterrestrial race communicating with them. I had experienced no such race yet.

Hopi spirituality defines a reality with multiple levels, not dissimilar to string theory or the multiverse theory. The Hopi believe that in the past worlds were destroyed and the Hopi were given a portal to go through to walk into the new world, those who were chosen to survive. In the modern twenty-first century it's difficult for rational westerners to engage native spirituality, but that's only because we've sealed up the doorway of the imagination.

Of most interest to me when I did my native research on the State of Arizona were the stories about the mountains closest to me, the Estrella Mountains. These are not the most noted mountain ranges for paranormal activity in Arizona. The most noted are the Superstitious Mountains. The Estrella Mountains are known for portals. The native lore speaks about portals opening up and what we might call gods coming through. The stories of portals abound in Arizona. It's hard to say what a portal is. It's hard to say what creates a portal. It's hard to say what sustains a portal. All I can do is give you my understanding. I'm not a shaman. I'm not a scientist. However, I am a man who has lived with multiple portals on his land and even inside his home.

A portal is a gateway between two or more worlds. It can be a gateway between more than two worlds. It is literally an opening up of our reality and an entrance way into another reality, or, conversely, an entrance from that other reality into our reality. Portals abound in our own storytelling. *Alice in Wonderland* is a perfect example of a portal. Even magicians who talk about mirrors are alluding to a way of creating a portal from a mirror.

The desert was a deeply fascinating place for me. There are people who become absorbed in the lore of the Arizona desert and mountains and do workshops and hiking tours, explaining the history and mystery surrounding various mountain ranges in Arizona. The stories of high weirdness go back through all of the culture, the native culture, the Spanish, the Jesuits, and now me, representing the latest people here on the land, the Americans. It's also interesting to note that every native culture in the world has a creation story in which the human race is seeded here. They do not believe in evolution. They believe we came here through something like the portals and that we were told to live here and develop ourselves here.

Deserts seem to be an integral part of human religious mythology. The Arizona desert is full of paranormal activity. I can attest to this after living here for two and a half decades. I am also forced to contemplate other desert cultures, like the people of the Middle East, and specifically the Jews. Many have made the connection between the Elohim and extraterrestrials, noting that the Jews refer to the gods in the plural rather than one creator. There is also the story of Jacob's fiery wheel. The entire Torah may be read as a communication between a seated human race and another race from another dimension. I don't allow the idea of extraterrestrials to interfere with my notion of a singular divine creator. If the human form has been tinkered with at the level of DNA, and we are in fact the creation of a superior species, it still doesn't explain the spirit. The other great desert culture that comes to mind is Egypt. They were also a splendid and mystical culture. The idea of portals abound in Egyptian culture. Some attest that the pyramids themselves are portals. In the world of science fiction and popular imagination, the line is already drawn between the ancient Egyptians and extraterrestrials through the television series Stargate, which commenced with a movie of the same name several decades ago.

The desert is a mysterious place. The desert of Arizona is an especially mysterious place. Many professional guides in Arizona will not take tourists into the Superstition Mountains after dark. Some of the locals call them the murder mountains. There is more death and craziness associated with the Superstition Mountains than almost any other place in Arizona. It begins with the lost Dutchman's gold. A German named Jacob Waltz told people that he found a large gold deposit in the Superstition Mountains, and he told a woman named Julia Thomas where it was. He stayed in a boarding house she ran in Phoenix. She had taken care of him for a number of years and he felt beholden. Ever since that rumor got out, adventurers have been going to the Superstition Mountains to try and find their fortune, but most of them just find their own deaths. Couple this with multiple stories of encounters with unknown beasts and monsters at night, some of them flying, and most people just stay clear of the Superstition Mountains.

Chapter 10

Men in Black

I became quite active on Gersten's website, the CAUS website. I started to write and publish short excerpts about my experiences on the ranch. I told about my wife levitating, the grays in the house, car keys materializing above my head in the air and dropping on me, the animal deaths, and everything else that I could think to include. The response was quite good. I was a first-hand source. That is gold in the UFO world. People have an innate understanding of when they're being lied to, and people, no matter how educated or unsophisticated, intrinsically know there is something wrong with a whole host of retired military people dominating the exopolitics world. So my stories were very well received.

I began to receive communication from all over the world. The phone would ring. I would answer it. The person on the other end would introduce themselves as a famous psychic from Paris, or Spain, or another part of the United States, or any part of the world, and they would begin to tell me things about the ranch. I was told that my ranch sat above one of the largest freshwater aquifers in the United States, and in fact, it is true. There is an enormous freshwater aquifer underneath me. I was told that there was a portal on my property. Not knowing what a portal was, I asked. It was explained to me that a portal was a doorway between dimensions, or what I might understand as time and space. The portal had been there for thousands of years. There was little or no understanding of where it came from, at least at this early stage of my investigation and communication with the world that began to take interest in my story. The portal was not only between locations, it was also a time anomaly. This meant that the portal could take beings from one time to another. I was told by several of these psychics who randomly called me from distant locales in the world that this was unique, and not a typical portal. I didn't feel lucky. They didn't know what it was like to live at the ranch.

I didn't know what to make of all this stuff. I mean, just imagine me, puttering about the ranch, working on a Harley-Davidson or an old 72 Chevy pickup truck, doing a full restoration, going into the house to get a glass of iced tea, and hearing the phone ring, answering, and getting another person on the other end of the phone from another part of the world, telling me that they're psychic and telling me about the place where I live. Put yourself in my shoes. Honestly, it all got to be a bit much.

I did note the strange coincidence of the phone line becoming a major source of information, given that the installation of the phone line was my first history of the property from a Buckeye resident, the brave soul who finally took the installation contract with Southwest Bell. Now the phone line was bringing me information from all over the world, from people who could allegedly see into these other dimensions of time and space that the rest of us are blocked from due to the gross nature of our senses and our mind dominating our perception. The phone line had worked for me.

I made a few friends in the community, outliers like myself who lived in the unincorporated Municipality of Rainbow Valley, people with their plots of land, living the same way I was. I can corroborate what the psychics told me — that the *phenomenon* on my ranch, in particular, was vastly superior to any other locale around me — is true. Some of my neighbors were experiencing the lights in the sky, and they did have a few bizarre things happen at their properties, but nothing compared to what Joyce and I were going through at Stardust Ranch.

I started to learn a lot more about the world of UFOs and extraterrestrials, and I started to meet more of the players involved. All of this stemmed from my initially reaching out to Captain Robert Collins. In certain circles, my story was a tier-one story. A tier-one story is a story with direct contact with UFOs repeating. I started to draw a lot of attention.

In the world of UFOs attention is not always a good thing. You indeed meet other experiencers like yourself, and it's an opportunity to commiserate and share stories and heal to a certain extent, but you also bring officialdom into your life. I can tell you unequivocally that the greatest source of disinformation on UFOs is coming from the United States Government. Everything they do is meant to obfuscate. Remember, government at an etymological level means to govern the mind from the Latin *mente*, which means mind. It's impossible for a government that does not have the support of the people to control a large population without fear, tyranny, and secret police, as was the case in some of the communist countries in Eastern Europe, or control is maintained through a collective fairy tale that everybody wants to believe because it's convenient and not believing it would raise too many uncomfortable questions.

My reputation as a restoration man for old cars, trucks, and motorcycles was getting quite good as well. Orders were coming in from all over Arizona and from out of state. It was good to keep busy during these times. The last thing you want to be is inactive when you have a lot of stuff to think about that is unpleasant. So I was very grateful for the work. I was also able to supplement the income at the ranch so that we could get the things that we needed.

The activity at the ranch continued as normal, or what we had come to define as normal after more than ten years of living on the ranch. The abduction attempts stopped after the AK-47 incident. At least we thought they stopped at the time. Joyce was no longer floating down the hall and out of the house through the wall. I guess that was a good thing, all things considered at Stardust Ranch. Things were still going missing in the house, and other *usual* nonsense was continuing. It had been a while since one of my animals was killed. I was very grateful for this. I guess you could say I slipped into a kind of routine. I didn't go out into the desert in the Jeep as much as I used to. Those days I was going out maybe once a week. Most of my time was spent in my workshop.

There were, however, new events happening. One of the strangest was what I call the Michelin Man. There was an advertising campaign, not sure what decade it was, but it featured the Michelin Man, which appeared to be a man made out of molded marshmallows, and all white. It was an ad campaign dreamed up by a bunch of goons for a tire company — Michelin Tires. If you remember the advertisements, the Michelin Man appeared quite tall, quite thick through the center, very much like the giant marshmallow man at the end of the first *Ghostbusters* movie.

One night I was outside tending to some chores in the stable. I happened to look over my shoulder behind the ranch, out into the desert, and I saw a figure walking. It had the shape of a human being, meaning that it walked erect on two legs and had arms swinging beside it, but the gait was different than a human being. It almost looked like that gait you see in all the old Bigfoot grainy video. It stood anywhere between ten and twelve feet high, at least that's what it appeared to be off in the distance. I would say it was about a quarter of a mile away, just walking across the desert.

Now, this may sound strange, but I didn't get all worked up about it. I didn't stop what I was doing in the stable. I didn't run back into the house to grab a camcorder. Nor did I walk out to get a closer look at whatever the creature was. I had made my peace with the ranch. Odd things were going on. I wasn't the creator and definer of all reality. Those days were behind me — the simple human arrogance of running out and attacking something you don't understand. It wasn't right on my land, so I didn't care what was going on out there. Live and let live, I figured.

However, Just like the grays, when something happens once, and when it happened so that a human being was aware of it, that is to say, there was a witness, it seemed to happen more frequently after that first witnessing. I started to see the large lumbering creature, the Michelin Man, on a more regular basis. It was like he had joined the cast of this *Twilight Zone* episode that was Stardust Ranch and kept coming back in a recurring role. It also started to get a little bit closer to the ranch. This caused me some concern. On one particular occasion, it was quite close to the home. I decided that enough was enough. I went into the house and I grabbed an AK-47 with a banana clip. I came back out and the creature had not withdrawn, and it appeared to have no sense of what was coming, no sense of danger, and it was encroaching on my home. I opened fire. Neither the noise nor the bullets deterred the creature whatsoever. I might as well have been tickling it rather than shooting it with an AK-47. To this day, I continue to see the Michelin Man periodically. I managed to see it close up on a few occasions and it looked like it was made of Brillo Pads.

Midday Visit

I can't remember exactly when it was, except to say it was sometime in the year I really went public, sometime when I started posting a lot on the web, and sometime when I started going on Internet radio and Coast-to-Coast. I think this would have been around 2008. But sometime around that time, I had a very strange encounter.

It was about midday. One of my nearby neighbors had driven over in his pickup truck and we were having a beer in the backyard. I had all my guns out on the picnic table. I had laid out a tablecloth to make sure none of the screws went through the crevices in the wood, and I was giving them a good cleaning. At that time I had somewhere between ten and fifteen guns.

It's a whole afternoon to clean them all. Any of you who collect guns know what I'm talking about. You have to break the guns down a little bit, scrub the chambers, and oil and polish. I enjoyed doing it. It took my mind off things. My neighbor, who will go unnamed in these pages, dropped by because he wanted a few tips on cleaning and maintaining his weapons as well.

So while we were there, drinking a few beers, listening to the radio, and cleaning the guns, a dark-colored SUV pulled up in front of my laneway. It parked about ten feet back from the entrance to the laneway. Two Men in Black suits got out. I know what you're thinking: You can't be serious. I am being serious. The two men, about average height, walked shoulder to shoulder the ten feet to the large iron gate that was closed. It was like a big cattle gate that stood about ten feet high made of solid metal bars. Now most people looking to get my attention would stand there and wait until I addressed them or walked down the laneway to talk to them, or, if they were impatient, they might yell out to get my attention. Cops do that. It's a power thing. These gentlemen walked right through the gate. Now I fully realize what I just said. They walked through the gate like the gate was made of cigarette smoke. I couldn't believe what I was seeing, but remember, what I was willing to believe had greatly amplified in the time I had been living at Stardust Ranch. My neighbor was speechless. He kept looking at them and then looking back at me. He had heard some of the stories about my ranch, and I had told him quite a few stories as well. I had no explanation for what was going on and I wasn't able to tell him anything. The two Men in Black suits each wore sunglasses and black fedora hats. With God and my neighbor as my witness, everything I am saying right now happened. They walked down the long hundred yard laneway. Their footsteps made dust on the dirt. I remember thinking, how come their feet are solid enough to kick up dust from the dirt laneway but they passed right through a metal gate? My neighbor was as mute as stone. I think he might have even been in some kind of shock. They stopped about six feet in front of me. My neighbor was behind me sitting at a picnic table full of guns. I had noticed that the black sedan they came up in had government issued black plates. It was just completely surreal. There was something off about their skin. It was like uncooked chicken skin, pale and clammy.

I said, Can I help you, gentlemen?

One of the Men in Black stepped in closer, so that he was about a foot from my face. He looked me right in the eyes and said, You're John Edmonds and you're going to stop publishing articles on Peter Gersten's CAUS website.

I said, Excuse me?

He repeated exactly what he had said the first time in the same pitch, like I was hearing an audio recording replayed.

You're John Edmonds and you're going to stop publishing articles on Peter Gersten's CAUS website.

With that the Men in Black turned around and started to walk down the laneway. My neighbor and I watched them walk the entire laneway and once again pass right through the metal gate at the roadway. They got into their sedan and drove away.

My neighbor waited about ten minutes after they left and then he left. He was shaken. We passed the usual stupid questions — Did that really just happen? Did they walk right through that gate? Did you see the skin? What was with that voice? — before his departure. It was events like this that garnered me a reputation in Rainbow Valley. But people had to be careful about what they said. They could end up looking crazy trying to describe something that happened at my property, like the Men in Black.

While working on this book with Bruce, we spent hours discussing how to tell the story. More specifically, how could we draw a circle around this story to give it a whole body so that it didn't just read like a series of interconnected vignettes of the paranormal? We both decided that we wanted to take our best shot at trying to describe what is going on on this planet, what is going on with the human race, and what is happening with our minds and the powers that be on this planet in their ability to make us look foolish and stupid when we try to describe things that happened.

First, let me be clear. What Dwight D. Eisenhower called the military-industrial-complex is now the military-industrial-entertainment-complex. That means that a lot of the ideas that Hollywood and the TV studios get are from the CIA, from NASA, the NSA, and from the deeper pockets of government that exist without any public lettering or signage whatsoever, and believe me when I tell you that such agencies that go undocumented do exist.

So why would they do this? They do it because they understand something that human beings don't understand about our consciousness as of yet. At the basic level of consciousness there is a rift between the real and the fictive. But at the level of pure experience, there's no difference between dream and reality. So by that rationale, if they make a movie called *Men in Black*, and make a comedy about it, everybody who seriously goes onto the public stage to talk about an encounter with the Men in Black looks foolish.

But it's more than that. The human race has a collective unconscious. In Latin it is referred to as the *spiritus-mundi*. This collective unconscious allows us to experience reality collectively and then communicate with each other. The vast majority of human beings are completely unconscious of it. That's why it's called the unconscious. We are all highly intuitive beings as well. The deepest parts of human consciousness communicate to us through our intuition. When something builds up in the collective unconscious it can be brought out collectively by what the Greeks called a catharsis. Catharsis is achieved when very strong and sometimes repressed emotions are released from a human being. The Greeks recognized that these feelings could be pulled out of human beings by drama. They created the Greek tragedies. What the entertainment component of the military-industrial-entertainment-complex does is provide false catharsis. If the collective unconscious is building an understanding of something along comes a movie that draws the emotions out and attaches the mind to the concept that first defines it. This means that every time somebody hears Men in Black they think of Will Smith and Tommy Lee Jones. They think of comedy. They think of everything that isn't serious. This is another chapter in the deep understanding of the human mind that is used to manipulate us, government propaganda through Madison Avenue and advertising and public relations, but it goes far deeper than that. As I said earlier in this story, psychiatry is the only medical art that is used against us in contravention of the Hippocratic Oath. If the average person truly understood the level of mind control going on in First World countries, and especially in the United States, there would be a bloody revolution in the streets tomorrow.

Part IV

Fighting Back

Chapter 11

Samurai John

Everything I have described in this story so far did not stop. We thought the abductions stopped, but they didn't. The negative energies that caused my erratic rages did not stop. The sightings of the grays didn't stop. There were other things going on as well, things I haven't mentioned in this story so far, mainly because I don't want to confuse people. What changed was my ability to cope with what was going on. The newest things in our lives, repeated often enough, become normal, the new normal. I could feel the gray energy sneaking up on me, but I didn't allow myself to become frustrated or angry. I tried to coexist with it, to transcend it. I was successful in good measure. It was my new normal. I had been living with it for over a decade by that point.

I believe everything in this life is learned by experience. The concept of faith is not lost on me. Faith is the belief that it all has meaning. I believe human beings should have faith in themselves, and we should have faith that our lives have meaning. We don't really know what we are at this point in history, not collectively anyways. They say everything in life has a silver lining, that if you have a lot of bad things happen then something good has to come to counterbalance it. The Taoists were the first to introduce this duality concept way before Carl Jung. They called it yin and yang. There had to be something I was learning at the ranch, and something I was learning in the best possible way, by experience.

We initially took a huge hit financially by me stopping my counseling business. I've never gone back to counseling since that early decision on the ranch. The few things I had done to help supplement the bills in the house, restoring old cars and motorcycles, mainly Triumphs and Harley Davidsons, was good, but I wanted to do more. I believe in doing things. I believe our ideas represent our unmanifest future.

How we deal with our ideas and inspirations define our lives. I started a non-profit animal sanctuary and took in horses that needed homes, *Hopeful Hooves*. We started to get horses from people who couldn't care for them anymore. I was a little haunted by the abandoned horses in the desert. It never really left my mind. I wanted to find a way to ensure horses didn't end up in the desert, horses that had been raised on ranches, horses that were accustomed to being fed and watered. It bothered me a lot that horses were abandoned in the desert. So I opened the shelter with Joyce's consent, started a small marketing campaign, and took donations for these abandoned horses.

I don't believe in accidents. I don't believe in coincidence. In my book, coincidences are almost always misinterpreted reality. A coincidence is always trying to tell us something. This might sound strange from a person going through what I was going through at the ranch, but remember what I said, I'm using my words very carefully — I believe experience is the best teacher.

I had a lot of time to think while I was out in my workshop. I was constantly trying to put a picture together in my mind, constantly trying to understand what was going on at the ranch. My mind settled on the idea that there was a dimension right beside ours. Things in that dimension could experience and see everything that was going on in our dimension but we could not see and experience their dimension with our five senses and mind. However, we had ways of knowing it was there. There were the moods that I spoke about earlier in this story. The incredibly negative and angry moods I would get myself into when I was at the house.

Being a former social worker who specialized in PTSD and addictions, and being capable of self-analysis to the degree that anybody is, I concluded that there was nothing going on in my own life that was creating these moods, no big change in diet, no chemical influence from the water, and nothing that would provide any kind of a physiological connection between temperament and cause, therefore, I concluded that my moods were a product of living next to this dimension, which, for some reason, had a much stronger presence at my ranch. The gray aliens could affect human moods, thinking, and behavior.

I fashioned a working hypothesis in my head where this was the case. There was some form of energetic reason why the ranch was such a way station or bus terminal for phenomenon from the fourth dimension. Now, as I said earlier in the story, I began to do a lot of research about the extraterrestrial phenomenon. There was no end of books to be found at used book stores in and around the Buckeye area and Phoenix. As I said before, it was something of a hotspot for extraterrestrial activity and discussion. I read *Fire in the Sky*, the Travis Walton abduction story. However, I remain a little bit doubtful because Walton had been a lifelong UFO enthusiast before he got abducted, and it just seemed to me like he was poisoning the whole experience.

One of the hardest things to get my head around as I worked on the Harleys and cars in my shop, was the idea that some portion of the dead, the human being who had left their bodies, who did not go to a higher and better place, was skulking about in some kind of nether world that was populated by extraterrestrials, and here I am referring to the young Mexican boy who killed himself himself in the house.

Perhaps absent the physical form and the biological energy we generate while physically alive, the disembodied humans were not bothered and capable of cohabitating with extraterrestrial life in the other dimension. In a weird way, the whole process of life became more understandable to me living on the ranch. This was the beginning of the dividend, the yin and yang that the Taoists spoke about.

I began to understand that physical life was just one form of life, and that energy never died, as Einstein stated, it just changed form, and somehow, in some way, consciousness persisted. An aspect of the individual persisted after the death of the physical body. Maybe not the entire personality and all of its discernment, but the tendencies of the being persisted after death.

As much as the experiences at the ranch were disconcerting, to say the least, there were some benign coincidences. The coincidences manifested in something entirely benign, but I'm getting ahead of myself. I will get to them in their proper place in this story. In the beginning, I would come across information that was extremely useful to me. I remember coming across the work of Robert Monroe. He was a pioneer in research about out of body experiences. He documented them in a book called *Journeys Out of the Body*.

He followed that first book with two sequels, the last being *Ultimate Journey*. Monroe zeroed in on the concept of frequencies. He claimed that certain sounds could create a mood in a person, either a very good feeling or a very bad feeling. He also believed that sound was able to create a dimensional doorway through which an aspect of the human being could leave the body. He claimed to have done this numerous times. His work was formalized in an institute called The Monroe Institute. It persists to this day. They deal with hemi-sync technology which aims to make the left and right sides of the brain operate in unison.

He also documented his journeys out of the body. He came to the conclusion that the human race was creating energies that were consumed by non physical entities, or entities outside of our time-space frequency. Essentially, he postulated that we were only at the top of the visible food chain, but the food chain went into these other dimensions where aspects of the human being exist. I am open to the idea of an immortal or divinely created part of the human being, only I prefer to know something rather than believe it.

Here is the mission statement of The Monroe Institute.

Our Mission

The Monroe Institute advances the exploration of human consciousness and the experience of expanded states of awareness as a path to creating a life of personal freedom, meaning, insight, and happiness.

The Monroe InstituteÂő (TMI), a 501(c)(3) nonprofit education and research organization, is a preeminent leader in human consciousness exploration. TMI is devoted to the premise that focused consciousness contains the answers to humankind's questions. Through the use of specific binaural beat technology, education, research, and development, TMI has been advancing the experience of individuals in the exploration of targeted and expanded states of awareness for close to 50 years.

Monroe was a laughingstock in the world of psychiatry when he went public with his first book. I commend his courage for going public. At the time, we were nowhere near the public discussion we have now on consciousness. There was no new age movement, no exopolitics, no advanced physics postulating multiple realities, at least not at the level of popular culture, no books or radio shows like Coast-to-Coast, just Monroe going public with his experiences.

I didn't have his courage, at least not back then. I dreaded going public with my story. I thought about what my former colleagues in mental health would think — Edmonds went out to live in nature and went crazy. We are all bound to this social consciousness to some degree. Nobody wants to be the pioneer for fear of ridicule.

The first person out with something new and unknown is a social punching bag. If you get big enough they'll be doing jokes about you on late night talk shows. The absurdity of that being my fear back then is only now funny. It took me years to get to this point. It's funny because I had really frightening things going on — aliens, violence upon my body, my wife levitating, assumed abductions, and a gray alien brained with a baseball bat — and my fear was *what people would think*. That's the power of social consciousness, the group think, the tribe.

We continued to have experience with the gray aliens. It was as though once they were discovered they were much more likely to allow themselves to be seen, or, at the very least, not as worried about being seen. I have the feeling that a big part of the power of this fourth dimension, or what some esoteric cartographers call the *lower* fourth, is the fact that human beings don't know about it. There is a man named Jerry Marzinsky breaking new ground in mental health.

Marzinsky worked in mental health for four decades, mainly with paranoid schizophrenics, and much of his work was done in the penal system. He believes schizophrenia is a lie, that the voices are not auditory hallucinations, and that the individuals are breached, where breached means that the membrane around us, what some call the aura, is weak and entities get into the afflicted individual, who is then placed on a regimen of anti-psychotic pharmacy that hurts rather than helps him. Marzinsky conducted multiple non-normative interviews with incarcerated schizophrenics in which he opened the discussion with the patients to the possibility that the voices were real. The response was affirmative. Many of the patients confirmed what Marzinsky suspected, and the patients began to describe a reality in which they were cohabited with groups of beings who were deceased human beings.

The rule on the other side was that the world of the living could not know these disincarnate beings were possessing the living, who were assumed to be mentally ill. If the human race came to the realization this was the case then the dead would be vacated from their hosts, and that was not an outcome they wanted. Much like the bruising and marking and branding Joyce and I went through, many of Marzinsky's patients showed him injuries given to them while they slept. Of course Marzinsky is a laughingstock, but I think he's on to something, a new frontier of human understanding that when realized and acted upon by the human race will herald a new age of mental health care.

I too have come to the belief that there is an aspect of this fourth dimension and the inhabitants therein that relies on human ignorance. Perhaps they have some kind of symbiotic relationship with the living that depends on the living believing they don't exist. However, once the secret was out at the ranch, the gray aliens seemed far less concerned with making themselves hidden. I started seeing them in the day more and more. The violence and chaos in the house, like the rattling around in the kitchen, and the stuff disappearing, abated for a while. It was almost as if we'd come to some sort of a truce with them, but it didn't last forever.

The next animal slaughter happened. One of my most beautiful horses was eviscerated. I found it in the stall in the morning. It had been fine and healthy when I went to bed. When I woke up it was just something of a husk of what it was the night before. And again, just like the Rottweiler, there had been no commotion, no sound, no warning in the middle of the night. This was an astounding feat for the aliens, beyond what we humans could do.

When an animal that is part of a social group, like dogs or horses, is being attacked, the rest of the group is quite vocal in their defense, making all kinds of noise to bring some kind of aid to the situation, lacking any other kind of recourse to stop what's going on. Not so with the animal evisceration. The only way I can describe it is to say that the remaining animals were narcotized somehow, but that would be looking at the whole phenomenon from our human perspective.

Who knows what they're capable of doing from the fourth dimension. If they could affect my mood and make me into an angry and raging lunatic in the middle of the day while being alone in the house, what could they do to a less developed mammal like a horse or a dog?

Whatever truce might have existed between myself and these aliens, was over after the evisceration of my beautiful horse. I thought of nothing else other than going to war with these creatures. A couple weeks before Christmas I was down around Phoenix, just outside the city limits, doing a little bit of shopping in the middle of the day. I was enjoying a little off-ranch time with myself and two of the dogs. I was following a pickup truck packed beyond safe capacity, I mean the guy's truck was overflowing. I considered calling the sheriff, but I had enough on my plate with the ranch. I was keeping a safe distance behind him because I was half expecting something to fall off the back of his truck. I could see that he had a Christmas tree packed in there but the rest of the stuff I couldn't quite make out.

Sure enough, a ways down the road, we hit a little bump and some things were discarded from his truck. He was completely unaware of it. I honked my horn but he didn't stop. I pulled over and gathered the stuff off the road. In an unbelievable twist of fate, one of the things that had fallen off the truck was a vintage samurai sword inside the scabbard. I couldn't believe it. I'm no expert on swords, but this seemed like something that was made with some care and attention, not a manufactured replica. I didn't get the man's license plate and was therefore unable to call him, but I want to assure you that I did speed off down the road and try and catch up with him to return what I considered to be a fairly costly piece of personal memorabilia that he'd lost on the road. Buddy had all but disappeared and I couldn't find him. So I inherited a samurai sword.

Joyce came home early that night. There was no second job during the month of December. I prepared a lovely meal for us to enjoy. It was rare that we had quality alone time. Joyce was avoiding the house. I felt like the man the Southwest Bell installer told me about, the guy who built the place, the guy whose wife didn't want to live there. The phenomenon of the house was still ninety percent experienced by me and ten percent experienced by Joyce. She was no stranger to what was going on, but given her relative absence from the house, except for sleep, there was nowhere near the same level of activity in her life.

I'd begun to avoid quiet time with my wife. Whenever we became relaxed, whenever we forgot what was going on at the ranch, she asked if I had changed my mind about moving. There was no changing my mind. I was dug in like Butch and Sundance fighting the Bolivian Army. I've changed a lot in the two plus decades I've been living at the ranch. My sixty year old self doesn't agree with my thirty-seven-year-old self, but we are who we are at each stage of our life, and back then I was obstinate and proud.

After dinner, we were enjoying a coffee and some small talk at the kitchen table, when I got up to go and get what I had found on the road, what had fallen off the pickup truck. I walked back into the kitchen and held the scabbard out in front of me.

What's that? Joyce asked.

I pulled the beautiful blade out of the scabbard.

Oh my God, she said. Where did you get that?

It fell off a truck, I said.

Chapter 12

Mortal Combat

The greatest revelation I had at the ranch was that human beings are not alone. The human mind is the enforcer of reality, but it's not always accurate. The mind is excellent for giving us the basic facts of where we live. Our mind tells us what we can and cannot do. It sets the primary laws of physics for our bodies as we exist in this three-dimensional reality. All of our sciences are based on memory, sequencing, foundation, and conceptualization, but there are things that we experience in which the mind operates as an obstacle not an aid.

If I say to you that we are not alone as sentient beings in this fluid reality, you might believe that you're capable of accepting that, but really you're not. None of us are. The mind enforces its reality. It can engage things outside its reality as concepts. Concepts precede experience. They are models of reality not yet experienced. Sentiment is a concept of feeling, not the feeling itself.

The American poet Wallace Stevens said, *Sentimentality is a failure of feeling*. In my thesis here, concepts are a failure to experience. Gray aliens phasing in and out of reality is something the mind will deny. The eyes can see it, but the mind will still deny it. The mind requires a context. It's almost like a database. Databases require the structured query language (SQL) to communicate. The mind has its own unspoken language based on habits, norms, and concepts. The language of the mind is context.

If you have an experience that the mind has no language for, the mind can't process it. It doesn't go into the database. I know this sounds harsh, but it's the truth. We've all seen things put right in front of us that we have not been able to assimilate. It happens every day. Psychiatry and psychology are schools of medicine. However, The vast majority of the psychology used by our society is used to manipulate and harm human beings. It was Sigmund Freud's nephew, Edward Louis Bernays, who started the first public relations firm on Madison Avenue in New York.

When you stop and think about this it's clearly immoral. Psychiatry and psychology fall under the Hippocratic Oath, which is do no harm. The oath does not actually say those words. They are a colloquial summation of the oath, but they are correct in spirit. Manipulating you into buying something that you do not need, that is not good for you, that is not good for the environment, that is not good for the human civilization on this planet, is doing harm. A case could be made that psychiatry has done the most harm to the human population of all the sciences in the twentieth century because it allows human beings to do things without realizing what they've done.

Bernays wrote the in his main work, *Propaganda*:

> The conscious and intelligent manipulation of the organized habits and opinions of the masses is an important element in democratic society. Those who manipulate this unseen mechanism of society constitute an invisible government which is the true ruling power of our country. We are governed, our minds are molded, our tastes formed, and our ideas suggested, largely by men we have never heard of.... It is they who pull the wires that control the public mind.

Part of our evolution as a civilization has pitted two competing schools of mind control against each other. One is the government and one is the private sector, the world of banking and commerce. The private sector is telling us to buy all kinds of crap we don't need that pollutes the environment and encourages us to feel a certain way about ourselves. The government is coming in and saying that we need to reduce what we consume and that we need to be concerned about the environment which is becoming increasingly polluted. I certainly don't agree with climate change.

My understanding is that most of the climate change is cyclic and related to the sun. However, I do believe that human beings have started to live in an unnatural way and this unnatural way of living, begun in the western world, has now spread to the four corners of the world, and any population capable of undergoing the rigors of being mentally entrained in the university system that we pioneered — engineering, chemistry, biology, medicine, computer science — are now producing societies as toxic as ours.

The accumulated toxicity is becoming more than the world can bare. Even in the world of salvation there are a whole bunch of misdirects. We've all had our attention put on the rainforests. Sure, they are important, but they're not the big player. Eighty percent of the human race's oxygen comes from the plankton in the oceans. Our oceans are being destroyed and that oxygen supply is being depleted.

Those of you who think a *Green New Deal* is the way to go, let me point out that the cadmium in the batteries we use is the main pollutants killing the plankton in the oceans. The mineral components of electric car batteries are another environmental catastrophe waiting to happen. In my estimation the problem is the culture of convenience that crept up about a hundred years ago.

The United Nations is now telling us that the only way to survive is to move into mega-cities under the auspices of Agenda 2021 and Agenda 2030. We can certainly see this going on now. The mega-city has become the new norm in the world — New Delhi and its suburbs, Mexico City and its surrounding area, The greater Chicago area, The greater Toronto area. Tokyo — but all of these city states require massive transportation, energy, and they create massive physical and mental pollution.

They are the palette upon which the ideological descendants of Edward Bernays paint our context, which, in my analogy, means control of our minds. The natural way for human beings to live is spread out in smaller communities with human beings having a certain amount of space and nature around us. It was completely unnatural to jam us all into condominiums that go up into the sky in these dense and dark cities. In most of these North American and European mega-cities now, the cost of a bachelor condominium is somewhere close to a half a million dollars. You could buy a trailer of equivalent size and ten acres of land with a water supply for one tenth the cost, yet the latter is regarded as a moron and the former is regarded as sophisticated.

The condominium is a good economic investment. The trailer in nature with clean water is a good life investment. It always seems to come down to money or life. The city also makes us extremely susceptible to all of the government's hijinx, which, from my experience, is no less malevolent than the extraterrestrials themselves. We are being pastured like cattle. They use salt licks and some grains to get the cattle in the pasture. They use our desires against us to get us into the the cities, the human pastures.

We live under the belief that only our actions define us to other people and other beings and entities in reality, but the ranch told me that is not true. Whatever we human beings are, we straddle a number of realities, the first and most prominent being our physical existence, defined by our actions and our speech, but our interior lives are also part of a landscape that in its own way is public to these entities and beings, in the same way that our words and actions are visible and understandable by our fellow human beings in this three-dimensional reality we call our world. There is no privacy in evolved consciousness. Everything we think and desire is visible on these other dimensions. Everything we fear is known to them.

That was a gigantic step forward for me as a human being. I am eternally grateful to the ranch for teaching me this. The moods that I would get into were set off by an influencer that was not physical. Whatever these entities are at the ranch — the disincarnate human beings, of which we surely had more than one, and the aliens, of which we had only encountered the grays at this point — they had the ability to communicate in the human interior.

The only place I ever encountered anything even approximating the psycho-spiritual-material reality I was experiencing at the ranch was in the work of Carlos Castaneda, the infamous *nagual* of the southwest immortalized in a series of books. In fact, to this day, Castaneda is the most accurate literature not directly about gray aliens that described what was happening to me at the ranch. Castaneda died in 1998. His work has been packaged into *Tensegrity*, a series of courses that can be studied from the comfort of your mega-city condominium for monthly installments. It's a disgrace, like almost everything the money hungry ideological children of Edward Bernays create with their distortions and manipulations.

The Duel

I put the samurai sword under the bed in the master bedroom. The days of baseball bats were past me. It was a blood sport now. The line in the sand was the beautiful horse they destroyed. In my reading on animal mutilations, they usually took place in pastures. As I said earlier in this story, the farmers would go out in the morning and find a dead animal. In my case they did it right inside a stable. I had the distinct sense that what was done to my horse was done to traumatize me. It was done to intimidate me. It was done as an act of confrontation. I received the message.

I started to see the grays in all of their various stages. It is really one of the more remarkable things I've ever seen, watching them come from wherever they come from into our reality. Imagine someone peeking out from behind a shower curtain so that all you can see is their face. That's how the grays peeked into our reality at the ranch before they fully stepped into it. You would either see just the face or the head poke through and no body. I would be sitting on the sofa watching television with Joyce, and I would catch out of of my peripheral vision one of the grays peeking through. If I saw them they didn't step through. A few times I saw them peek through, without them seeing me, then I saw them step through. I can only describe it as some kind of real-world computer-generated interface, it was so astounding to watch.

Since the baseball bat to the head incident in the master bedroom, the grays had been less finicky about materializing. Once the code is broken, once a human being knows what's going on from this three-dimensional reality, they're not so big on keeping the secret anymore, and they really don't care if you see them. I'm not saying they go out of their way to be seen; it's just that they seemed a lot less preoccupied with being caught in the house.

I was in a constant state of vigilance. I had connected the change in pressure around me to the proximity of the grays, even if they had not materialized yet. I had learned how to control my thinking and not allow the influence of these entities to set me into a negative mood. I was looking for a confrontation. I considered the samurai sword to be an act of providence, some great act of fortune, the universe telling me to go to war, so I soldiered.

I do apologize for not being able to remember the dates, but remember that this is a story that spans two and a half decades for me. I believe this encounter was sometime around 2007. The story unfolded for me in major events. Once the event happened — the lights in the sky, the disappearing items around the house, Joyce levitating, the marks on our bodies, the animal mutilations, — it became a normal part of our experience at the ranch. The only exception was the Men in Black. They came a second time, but they did not become a regular occurrence at the ranch.

One day I was home alone. Joyce was at work. I was comfortably nestled into the sofa with a Pepsi, a Triumph motorcycle gas tank, and several grades of sandpaper. I had machines in the shop to do the grinding, but when it got down to the final work I liked to do it by hand. So sometimes I would just set up camp in the living room, lay down some newspaper to catch the grit the sandpaper took off, and relax in front of the television while I did some of the finer work on the motorcycle restoration.

I felt the pressure change around me. They were close by, but not yet visible. It was at these times that I would maintain absolute calm. The key was not to give them any emotional or mental indicators that you were aware of their presence. I had been working on this mental and emotional training for months. It was a Zen state of mind. I do believe they could pick up thought patterns if not outright read minds. Staying calm and focusing on what you were doing and acting like nothing was going on, including even your thinking processes, was key to success. I used my peripheral vision to glance around me. I changed the channel on the television to make them think that I was unaware.

Sure enough they appeared. I saw the first one poke his head out. They were in the sun room, a little glass room we had off to the side of the house. I had a clear line of sight from the living room sofa. It was about thirty feet away. I casually stood and walked to the bedroom. I bent down and grabbed the samurai sword from under the bed. I placed it on the inside of the door frame to the master bedroom. I then went back to the sofa and casually resumed what I had been doing, changing the television channel once again. This was all part of my cover.

A couple minutes later I saw three of them phase into the sunroom. I didn't move right away. I didn't look back, not even with my peripheral vision. After waiting about ninety seconds, I got up and went back to the bedroom. I grabbed the samurai sword. I went down a hallway that hid me. It would bring me out right at the sunroom without them seeing me coming. I unsheathed the sword. I glanced around the corner and the three grays were inside the sunroom. The sunroom screen door was open. I could charge right in with the sword and swing. I took a slow deep breath through my nostrils and charged. My stroke was perfect. I cut the head clean off one of the grays. The other two dematerialized immediately.

It turns out that they cannot dematerialize with their heads cut off. I had pummeled them with baseball bats, put bullets in them, and stabbed them in the past, but nothing had prevented them from phasing out of my reality, out of my reach, and safe from my wrath. The samurai sword changed all of that. Like some cheesy subtext in a horror movie, they were killed by chopping their heads off. I should point out at this juncture, that they always appeared in threes. There seemed to be one principal and two subordinates. I killed the principal. The two subordinates disappeared. This was a major error for a race of beings that wanted to maintain anonymity.

I say that they wanted to maintain anonymity because if it were anything else, the whole world would know they exist by now. So we can safely assume that part of their mission is clandestine, just like the occupying entities in the schizophrenics detailed by Jerry Marzinsky. They don't want their existence on this planet, or whatever sub plane frequency they exist next to us, becoming common knowledge in the human race. They do not want the collective consciousness of the human race working on them as a problem. Secrecy is part of their mandate. When I severed the gray aliens head, part of that secrecy was destroyed.

I picked up the two parts of the body and wrapped them in plastic, the head and the corpse. I put them in a large freezer we kept for meat. When Joyce got home that night she saw the mess, a brownish liquid on the walls and floor. I had no choice but to tell her what happened. It might sound weird, but by this point we were so accustomed to the ranch that nothing really struck us as weird anymore, so when I told Joyce I killed a gray with the samurai sword it took her about five seconds to digest and then she just nodded. Her only question was what did I do with the corpse.

The Alien Cadaver

The dead gray alien was in my freezer for some time. I literally didn't know what to do with it. Things continued on the ranch. Nothing really abated. The one thing that did happen was Joyce and I started getting consciously abducted by the grays. Abduction is something you become aware of after it has happened. Gray aliens have the ability to take all memory of something out of us. Most people who come to an understanding that they've been abducted do so through hypnotherapy. It remains in another part of the consciousness, separated from our waking mind. There are countless people on the planet who have been abducted and do not know it. I would say that the abduction phenomenon is widespread and spans most of the world, but it is heavily concentrated in the United States, and it is true that Arizona is a hotspot for UFO abductions, New Mexico as well.

I really didn't understand what I had done. I had killed what is ostensibly a sentient being. Given that the government does not officially recognize the existence of extraterrestrials, I seriously doubted that there were any legal consequences. There are no homicide investigations for dead extraterrestrials. Nonetheless, I had done something, something big, something uncommon. You have to understand that I was acting from the position of a man who was experiencing a home invasion. I saw my actions as no different than a man who shoots an intruder entering their house in the middle of the night.

With a dead gray alien in my freezer, I was faced with the uncomfortable responsibility of going public. Sure, a lot of people knew about my ranch. The Mormon Bishop knew. Many of the Buckeye locals knew. It was mainly a regional story back then, not so much an extraterrestrial story, more about a bizarre house with a bizarre history and a number of deaths associated with it, none of them alien. This was something else entirely.

I had reached out to the Department of Agriculture and to the Sheriff's Office and two other agencies regarding the death of my dog. It was nothing they hadn't heard before. Whatever the government knew about what was going on in Arizona. they weren't sharing it with the public. This has been a theme of extraterrestrial phenomenon in the United States since its inception. This is why the UFO world remains a counterculture relegated to the world of conspiracy and superstition, the tinfoil-hat world.

Now let me be clear here: going public in the UFO world doesn't mean that you're going to end up on the front of every newspaper just because you have a dead alien body. The world of UFOs is one of the most guarded and secret sub-cultures in the world, with the United States Government and military being one of the most active players in the widespread dissemination of disinformation related to UFOs. It's no coincidence that many of the big players in the UFO world are retired military and intelligence people. They were under strict orders while in service not to disclose information.

Many of them found their code of silence, the see no UFO, hear no UFO philosophy, a hard pill to swallow. Upon retirement many of these men and women become vocal proselytizers of the UFO phenomenon, believing that people have a right and a need to know that we're not alone on this planet, in this solar system. this galaxy, this universe, and other universes. Everybody has their own motivation for going public. For some people, it's just the idea of information this fantastical being restricted from the general public. Other people, coming from a deeper place in the military or intelligence community, may have a protection or security *crisis of conscience* based on what they know.

The only thing I can tell you for sure is disclosure is not disclosure, the government is misinforming you, and there is an active effort to thwart real disclosure. You could rent a truck with loudspeakers and drive all through Washington DC blaring your message and you still wouldn't end up on the front pages of newspapers and magazines around the world. The UFO world has been deliberately occulted by the mainstream media and by the powers that be in our world. There are any number of reasons for this, the one that strikes me as the most likely is that the government has had direct contact with UFOs, made arrangements and treaties with them, and those arrangements and treaties did not work out the way the government wanted, and now the government is left holding a bag of very dirty secrets that they don't want to own.

I went back to Captain Robert Collins, who I had not spoken with very much for quite some time. Maybe I was a little put off by the Men in Black, truth be told. I did lay off posting on Gersten's website as they had instructed. It's funny because at a mental level I had a defiant attitude, but in actuality I did what they told me to do. It might have been some kind of Jedi mind trick they played on me. I hadn't even thought it all through until the dead alien in the freezer.

The UFO world is populated with experiences. Very few people can aggregate those experiences into any kind of meaningful narrative, though. Add to this the high number of people in the UFO world who are former intelligence or military or military intelligence and the narrative gets even more muddled. Whenever you have a lot of govern-

114

ment and quasi-government people associated with anything what is going on is a controlled narrative. Very often the narrative is controlled not to deny the experience, because the experience cannot be denied, but to prevent any kind of meaningful aggregation of the experiences. Collins was a master of his craft.

He told wild stories about discs that had been found and reverse engineering going on and secret laboratories. It was like dim light going through a dirty diamond. There was no clear picture. I had the smoking gun. Collins was more interested in what I told him than anything he had ever heard before. I had an alien in my freezer, killed with a samurai sword. He had a very clear plan of action. We needed to get tissue samples to a doctor he knew, a Doctor Levengood in Michigan. Levengood was a biophysicist and crop circle researcher who was fascinated by the UFO world. We were going to run tests on the tissues and determine whether the DNA was part of the genomes on planet earth.[1]

Levengood's obituary [2] reads, in part, as follows:

Lefty" Levengood, a pioneering biophysicist and long-time resident of Grass Lake, Michigan (and the "L" in the original "BLT Research Team"), has died at the age of 88. Educated at the University of Toledo (B.S. in Physics and Mathematics, 1957), Ball State University (M.A. in Bioscience, 1961) and the University of Michigan (M.S. in Biophysics, 1970), Levengood worked as a research physicist at the now-defunct Institute of Science & Technology and the Dept. of Natural Resources at the University of Michigan from 1961 through 1970, after which he was employed as the Director of Biophysical Research and as a consulting scientist for various private-sector companies.

Because of his wide-ranging scientific curiosity he maintained a well-equipped laboratory at his home in Grass Lake, where he pursued a variety of interests and obtained multiple patents, several relating to seed germination and vigor

---

[1] MacDonald Note: The first time I tried to write this book, in 2012-2013, right around the time I was getting prepped to interview Dr. Levengood, he died. No record of his work with John Edmonds's samples exists except the material provided by Edmonds himself.

[2] http://www.openminds.tv/biophysicist-and-crop-circle-researcher-w-c-levengood-passes-1971/24370

and the development of new plant varieties through genetic transduction. He also authored more than 50 peer-reviewed papers published in professional scientific journals, including several in the preeminent journals Nature and Science, as well as in a diverse selection of other professional publications, ranging from The American J. of Physics and the J. of Applied Physics to The J. of Experimental Botany, The J. of Chemical Physics, The J. of Physics and Chemistry of Solids, Bioelectochemistry and Bioenergetics, The J. of Geophysical Research, to The J. of Insect Physiology and many others.

In December of 1990, after his wife Glenna had seen a TV crop circle show (which he then subsequently also watched), Levengood contacted Pat Delgado (one of the original British investigators of the phenomenon) and they arranged for Delgado to begin shipping plant samples and controls to "Lefty's" Michigan laboratory. Almost immediately Levengood began to find multiple anomalies in the plant samples from within the crop circles as compared to the control plants taken at various distances outside the formations (but in the same fields). In these early trial stages of his crop circle research some approaches were non-productive, while others began to build a consistent data set of abnormal changes characteristic of the crop circle plants.

He maintained a thirteen year interest in the crop circle phenomenon, electromagnetic energy, and UFOs. Collins and I contacted Levengood. He was excited by what we told him. He made a laundry list of tissue and *part* requests. I did exactly as instructed and sent everything by insured FedEx.

Chapter 13

Breaking The Fourth Wall

Theater and film have the concept of the fourth wall. If you look at the structure of an outdoor amphitheater that the Greeks used to perform in, its shape represented three walls. This was for acoustics. The actors' voices would pitch out into the stands. It was also to represent the reality space for the actors. If you've ever been to a modern theater production, there's a left wall, a right wall, and a back wall, the same basic structure of the amphitheater, the place for viewing. The fourth wall is the audience. The actors on the stage pretend the audience is not there. This is the strength of the drama. It takes place enclosed within its own reality and is watched live by an audience.

Breaking the fourth wall occurs when a actor on the stage or in a film directly addresses the audience. An example of this would be the film *Ferris Bueller's Day Off*. The central character addresses the audience directly numerous times throughout the film. Another example would be Woody Allen directly addressing the audience in *Annie Hall.*

I need to break the fourth wall as a writer. I, Bruce MacDonald, need to speak directly to you the reader to help you understand the story John and I are trying to tell. It needs to be stated that John's memory is not one hundred percent as far as the timeline goes. John and his wife Joyce have endured a superhuman level of stress, trauma, and terror. John is an unusual human being in his capacity to take abuse and keep going, perhaps some kind of flicker in his fight or flight response. The most difficult topic to broach while working on this book with John was the topic of abductions. We've already spoken about the blue-white beam coming from the saucer and Joyce levitating through the house to be taken on an abduction and John firing an AK-47 into the craft, but we have not spoken about of the abductions that were successful.

John and his wife underwent numerous abductions. Through regression hypnotherapy John recalled eighteen abductions. These regressions were done by a medical doctor who worked with the Department of Defense in Washington, specializing in post-traumatic stress disorder for combat veterans. The government is a part of John's story. They know he exists. They know what's going on with his ranch. His story has been verified as authentic six ways to Sunday. It would stand the scrutiny of any grand jury or any inquisition brought into force to prove or disprove the veracity of his claims.

A number of people that stayed at the ranch experienced phenomenon. Many of them attest to the phenomenon that goes on at the ranch. The popular television series, *Ghost Adventures*, did an episode at the ranch, episode twelve of season twelve, the only extraterrestrial story they have done. Many psychics have gone out to visit John and Joyce and stayed at the ranch for a week or so, all of them verify what John and his wife Joyce have been saying for over two decades.

In the many hours I spent with John recording conversations and putting together this story, I tried numerous times to get John to talk about the abductions, but it's a topic that he finds too personal to include in the book. Most people who have been abducted have a sense of privacy about the event that is akin to a rape survivor. There's something deeply personal about the abduction phenomenon.

The world of exopolitics has gone over this material in great detail. One of the most outspoken voices about the abduction phenomenon was Dr. Karla Turner. She had a PhD in English literature. She was one of the most articulate voices in the exopolitics community until her untimely death by cancer in 1995. She was only forty-eight. She captured the abduction phenomenon perfectly in a 1992 book published by Berkeley Press titled *Into The Fringe*. Dr. Turner lived with her husband in rural Arkansas, deep in the woods by a river in the mountains.

She also authored the book *Taken*, which inspired a television miniseries produced by Steven Spielberg, whether he accredits her or not. Spielberg's miniseries brings in the multi-generational aspect of abductions, which is undeniably the cornerstone of Turner's work. Dr. Turner states in her many lectures available on YouTube that she was not able to fully understand the abduction phenomenon until she engaged other abductees and interviewed them. She makes it very clear that trying to understand the abduction phenomenon from your own experiences alone will produce an incorrect picture of the phenomenon. John and Joyce Edmonds have never gone out into the world as abductees and discussed the abduction phenomenon that they have been through, nor, in my many conversations with John, did I get the sense that he had done an extraordinary amount of research into the abduction phenomenon.

When Dr. Turner did her work in the early nineties, the UFO community had not fully blossomed to the degree that it has now in the early twenty-first century. The History Channel was not doing a series called *Ancient Aliens*. People were not talking about the connection between native mythologies, Biblical references, and references in other scriptures, as extraterrestrial contact. Now they are.

One of the refreshing aspects of Dr. Turner's circumspection of the abduction phenomenon is that she didn't rest on any patented answers. She even refused to designate them as alien abductions, and stated as a matter of fact that nobody can say for certain whether these entities are extraterrestrial, interdimensional, originating on the earth, or a combination of the three or more. The injection of extraterrestrial into the narrative is an entirely human conjecture, or at least it was at the time that Dr. Turner was doing her work thirty years ago.

The human record shows interaction with nonhuman intelligent and individuated life forms in all civilizations. The Celtic people had their fairies and gnomes. The Chinese had their Dragons as did the English. European peoples had their angels and demons. Dr. Turner states the design of the abduction experience is done deliberately to leave no tangible evidence for a community response. In fact, the abduction phenomenon has all the hallmarks of a spiritual experience. It is no more possible for a third party to experience what an abductee experiences than it is for that same third-party to understand what Francis of Assisi was trying to describe as the result of his alleged mystical experiences.

I don't seek to define these things at an experiential level. I just don't know whether they are alien abductions or not. I do validate these experiences as part of the fourth wall that our reality has been constructed with. In the fourth wall of our reality we are the actors unaware we are on a cosmic stage and the break occurs when the producers and directors speak to us. The fourth wall in the human experience is our inner life. Until a human being has an awakening experience, the assumption is that the inner life is the product of the mind, the imagination, and all of the parts of us that constitute consciousness, and all of it is private and the sole experience of the individual.

These fourth wall experiences all have characteristics in common. The people who experience them, always alone, whether they be Moses talking to a burning bush, or Christ talking to Satan in the desert, or an abductee claiming that aliens were inside their head, all experience this breach of the human fourth wall, the subjective world is defined as having objective qualities. Normally this is defined as insanity. But what do you do when large groups of people from all over the world with nothing in common start to report a common breach of the fourth wall in their own minds in the form of alien abductions? How do you explain the commonality?

To stay with the insanity definition is to entertain the notion that mental illness, including common and similar hallucinations — gray aliens, examination tables, disks, blue-white lights — are viral, meaning they are contagious and pass from one person to the other. It's ludicrous, hence my *fourth wall* allegory. I need something to circumscribe the phenomenon, something that bridges the rational and the irrational, the subjective and the objective.

When you start to see it this way, that the inner and outer life are connected, that human consciousness directly interacts with reality in ways other than directing the arm to pick up a cup of coffee, then everything we know about reality gets turned upside down. This basic message of a human connection with everything around us has been given to us numerous times in so many different ways, shapes and forms they are too numerous to count. In our desire to stay within the womb of our imagination, the *private* world of our inner life, we individually and collectively rationalize that these things are various forms of fiction, mythology, fairy tales, religious scripture, or mystical experiences. The only form of human narrative to escape this death by rationalization is religious scripture, but that war rages on in the form of radical atheists like Richard Dawkins openly suggesting that religious belief is a form of mental illness.

The only place we find experiences even remotely similar to the ET world occur in the occult and spiritual domains. Vedic practitioners describe multiple planes of reality surrounding our physical reality, or interacting with our physical reality but outside of the fundamental frequency by which we apprehend physicality. It's already been described in this book that human hearing and human sight is a small bandwidth of all of the sound and light that is available to be perceived by finer instruments. Jesus Christ stated that the kingdom of heaven is within us. There are numerous references to a non-physical world in the Gospels — In my Father's house are many mansions: if it were not so, I would have told you. I go to prepare a place for you.[1]

The Quran tells us about another sentient species created by the same creator that made us that lives alongside us and can see us but we can't see them, the Jin. The Quran goes on to tell us that man was made from clay and the Jin were made from fire. All around us there are examples of human consciousness interacting with worlds that don't fit into the five sense and mind reality we all share entombed within our fearful rationality.

Naysayers Versus Pioneers

The twentieth and twenty-first centuries have seen a vigorous attempt the close the fourth wall in human experience. *Abducted: How People Come to Believe They Were Kidnapped By Aliens*, by Susan Clancy is an attempt to deny this fourth wall in human experience. Clancy is a cognitive psychologist who studied at Harvard, where she remains a Post-Doctoral Fellow. Harvard became a staging ground for whether the theater of life would allow the fourth wall in human consciousness. Another professor, John Mack, the Head of Psychiatry at the Harvard Medical School until his strange and untimely death by a drunk driver in 2004, was her antecedent and antipode.

Harvard became the litmus test for whether the formal scientific and academic world would accept alien abduction and take these people seriously or shut it all down as repressed memory resurfacing in adulthood. Mack published a book called, *Abduction: Human Encounters with Aliens*, in 1994. It is an odd twist of fate that one year after his accidental death a young, up and coming colleague at Harvard would publish a work which completely refutes his conclusions on alien abduction, making him look foolish and discrediting him as scientist in the field of psychiatry.

Again and again we see this battle for legitimacy, this struggle in academic and scientific circles for authenticity among experiencers, and

---

[1]John 14:2

again and again we see them reduced to casualties of mental illnesses or false memories. It's really quite a feat by officialdom to keep the fourth wall in human experience closed, and so long as officialdom does not recognize it, the experiencers are left to fend for themselves, struggling for dignity and credibility in a world that has labeled them insane at worst and marginalized at best. John Mack endorsing, or at least not dismissing, the phenomenon of human abduction, is perhaps the biggest nod ever from officialdom that the phenomenon is real, that it's happening to people, and we really don't understand what it is. He sums up his position perfectly in a BBC interview.

> I would never say, yes, there are aliens taking people. I would say there is a compelling powerful phenomenon here that I can't account for in any other way, that's mysterious. Yet I can't know what it is but it seems to me that it invites a deeper, further inquiry. [2]

Curiously, Mack never literally declared that aliens were real. He equated the abduction phenomenon with visionary experiences throughout the human history which he noted seemed to have fallen away at the beginning of the Industrial Revolution, so Mack gives us a kind of *fourth wall* explanation, splitting the difference between the experiencers and scientific empiricism. Although all credit should be given to Mack for even taking on the subject of alien abductions at Harvard, in the end he sort of watered it down to a kind of Joseph Campbell hero quest that was part of the spiritual traditions of the West, nonetheless, the abduction and exopolitics world has embraced him as validation.

The rest of the academic community, and especially the hallowed halls of Harvard, were not nearly as thrilled as the exopolitics community that a tenured professor — the head of Psychiatry at the Harvard Medical School — was writing on the nonsensical topic of alien abduction. In May of 1994 the Dean of the Medical School, Daniel Tosteson, set up a committee of colleagues to go over Mack's clinical work and investigation. Never before in the history of Harvard had a tenured professor been subject to this kind of investigation. The committee was headed by a medical doctor named Arnold Reiman. He was some kind of heavyweight, a professor of medicine and of social medicine at Harvard Medical School, and he edited the prestigious *New England Journal of Medicine*. The committee's draft report stated:

---

[2] http://news.bbc.co.uk/2/hi/uk_news/magazine/4071124.stm

To communicate, in any way whatsoever, to a person who has reported a 'close encounter' with an extraterrestrial life form that this experience might well have been real ... is professionally irresponsible.

If that wasn't enough, one year after his death by a drunk driver while giving a lecture in London, England, Mack's work is completely contradicted by his antithesis personality at the Harvard School of Medicine, Susan Clancy, who publishes her work on the topic.

Clancy completely dismisses and even ridicules the abduction theory as a literal phenomenon. According to her work, the abduction scenarios are the product of sleep paralysis and the use of hypnosis in the recovery of forgotten memories. She notes that all of the subjects reporting abduction phenomena had a previous interest in the paranormal and were invested emotionally in creating abduction memories.

It was a devastating blow for people who claimed abduction experiences. Clancy was quoted as saying the following as it regards the response of abductees to her work.

I can tell you most of them that have read the book are upset. I have to be honest with that. And I understand why, because what's happening in the book is I am presenting my own opinion, but I'm challenging their deeply held beliefs, beliefs that are very important to them. So they're angry, and I feel terribly about it.

She also, in agreement with her predecessor at Harvard, John Mack, gives a nod to religious belief and abduction experiences when she says the following:

All I would like to say is that in the same way that people find meaning in their religious beliefs and experiences, these people find meaning in their alien abduction beliefs and their alien abduction experiences.

And just like that, the promise of support for abductees from high up in the medical community was taken away. It was again relegated to the superstitious and nonsensical contortions of immature minds that didn't understand themselves and bizarre belief systems percolating in the unconscious. Curiously, Clancy's follow-up work was on childhood sexual abuse. The book was titled *The Trauma Myth: The Truth*

About Sexual Abuse Of Children And It's Aftermath. It was published in 2010. She states that the genesis of the book was research she was doing in the nineties which had her commence the interviewing of adult survivors of childhood sexual abuse. And by the timing of her books on the abduction phenomenon and childhood sexual abuse, we can assume a cognitive overlap in abduction and childhood sex abuse research. What Clancy overlooks, rather suspiciously, is the highly sexual nature of abductions.

Abductees report semen extraction, anal penetration, and feelings similar to those of a rape survivor, with violation being the principal trauma inducing emotion. In fact, it may easily be adduced that Clancy is postulating childhood sexual abuse as one of the main traumatic memories in the unconscious which fabricate abduction scenarios in adults. The parallels are present. Childhood sexual abuse happens in childhood. The abduction phenomenon usually begins with repressed memories resurfacing through some form of hypnotherapy and the hypnotized person going back to their *childhood* and identifying that as the time that the abductions began. What Clancy does not explain in her work, aside from an allusion to abduction seduction — many abductees fantasized about meeting aliens — is the commonality of the experience, the blue-white light beam, the operating table, and, in many instances, the presence of human beings in military uniforms. Perhaps Clancy sees the uniforms as some kind of sadomasochistic sexual fantasy. In any event, her work and her opinions do not explain the phenomenon of abduction. They dismiss it, which might have been Harvard's goal all along, the esteemed Ivy League institution wanting desperately to wash off the *stench* Mack put on them when he loaned credibility to the abduction phenomenon.

Finally, to be thorough in the vetting of this topic, many in the rather conspiracy-minded UFO world believe Mack was murdered. The circumstance of his death is quite odd. He was not crossing the street in London when struck. The car jumped the sidewalk and struck him. The driver was arrested, and he plead guilty to careless driving under the influence. Mack's family sent a letter to the court to be read during sentencing that asked for leniency, and expressing their conviction there was no malice on the part of the driver, certainly an act of heroic compassion and forgiveness on the part of the Mack family. Most people in a similar circumstance would seek the maximum penalty, if not for their own pain, then for the safety of the public, as alcoholic drivers don't often reform even after inflicting massive loss on others.

There's one final thing to address in looking at Harvard's foray and then rapid departure from abductions — sex. If we are going to talk about abductions then we have to talk about human reproduction. Many abductees report sexual interaction. Women report being impregnated. Men report having their seed extracted. At the center of this conjecture is the theory of an alien-human hybrid program. The women report having their fetuses taken before full term. There is no evidence they were ever even pregnant. However, they stand by their claims.

As you move deeper into the more paranoid world of conspiracy theories that conflate alien abduction with human agendas, we have a theory of genetic lines on the planet that host non-human beings. One example of this is the work of the British researcher, David Icke. He claims many of the powerful family bloodlines on the planet are reptilian-human hybrids. Fantastically, he, and others, claim these beings are capable of shape shifting between human and reptilian form, and, most curiously, they require or crave sex with children, especially prepubescent boys. There is no really clear explanation for this, however, some researchers, like the American YouTuber and lecturer, Kerry Cassidy of *Project Camelot*, postulate that what they want is an energy human beings have at the base of the spine, a psycho-spiritual energy called *kundalini* in Vedic texts, or what some refer to as *chi*, or *prana*, a life giving energy that yogis and Taoists, among others, attest heals, allows for supernatural acts and perception, and is particularly present in prepubescent boys. Some western researchers — certainly not in the halls of the Ivy League like Harvard — claim the human race is farmed by transdimensional entities for this energy. This was the conclusion of Robert Monroe discussed in a previous chapter. This is where he claims he heard the word *lush*, which is what the beings in Monroe's out of body experiences called the human energy being taken.

This aspect of the story might not be worth addressing if not for the high profile dismantling of child sex trafficking networks. Jeff Epstein procured child sex partners for the rich and famous. Photographs and air transit logs connect him to American presidents and British royals, thus bolstering Icke and Cassidy's conjecture that elites are mired in pedophilia. Now, as for an alien connection, the curious point of intersection is the work of Harvard fellow, Susan Casey, who tackled two main topics in her Harvard research — abductions and childhood sexual abuse. Her work on abductions is utterly dismissive and an insult to experiencers. Her follow-up work is a refutation of the idea that sex with children damages them, that, in fact, it is the realization in adulthood that society views them as having been violated and abused that causes the trauma, in essence, tying together alien abductions and pedophilia, a coincidence which cannot be overlooked.

Chapter 14

Bigelow and Bullets

With the increased notoriety of going public, albeit only in the rather esoteric and basement world of exopolitics, I came up on a lot of people's radars. This was somewhat helpful in getting guidance and understanding from other people experiencing similar things, but it was also extremely dangerous. I had already been warned by the Men in Black to stop talking in public about what was happening at my ranch. I didn't listen to them. I don't obey well. I've never been easy to scare. I was given mild caution by Captain Robert Collins and others I confided with. They did tell me there were a lot of forces working against disclosure. It's not like I wanted fame and fortune with my ranch.

When Bruce MacDonald was introduced to me in 2012 he seemed like a good fit for a book. Others had approached me over the years, but they had a vibe I can't quite describe, — creepy, opportunistic, and shady — Bruce was new to the field of exopolitics, not that interested in the book, and approaching it more as an act of service for Joyce and I. I knew he was the Frodo I needed to carry my ring to Mordor. He took eight years to write the book. The first time he tried the energy from the ranch found him and scared him off it. The ranch can do that. People who have come here report interacting with the energies years after they leave. You get tagged when you experience the ranch. You don't have to visit the ranch to get noticed by the energies and entities here. Bruce got noticed just writing the book. He went through the rage moods I had when I first moved here, and he had visitation even on his mountain ranch in Costa Rica, and all of it just by tuning his mind to the ranch through the act of writing the book.

The Maricopa County Sheriff's Department came to know me quite well. I was out in my work shed one day, the shed that the man at the beginning of the story — the monster killer with the machete in my laneway — said he lived in, working on a motorcycle, sanding and polishing one of the metal parts, when a large caliber bullet broke through the wood wall and whizzed past my head, exiting the wooden shack through the back wall, only the one bullet, no second round. I don't know how the person got the bullet so close to me without being able to see me behind the wall, but they did. I also don't know if it was a genuine attempt to kill me or just an attempt to scare me.

I would remind you at this point of the words from the Men in Black, *Your name is John Edmonds and you're not to talk about aliens on Peter Gersten's website anymore.* This felt like a follow-up to that conversation but with a different division of the US government speaking to me. When you're in the world of exopolitics and you're going public with information that the government doesn't want public, a lot of things are done to discredit, intimidate, and frighten you off your position. Many people have been frightened off of their positions.

There are probably more lost voices in the UFO world than those who form the body of voices that have been the chorus of this information for the last four or five decades. Most people just don't have the stomach for it. It's dangerous. It's harrowing. It's difficult to have a normal life and give security to your loved ones, and it's extremely frustrating. So what keeps me going? If I knew the answer to that I would tell you. I just will not give up. I drew my line in the sand early on. I believe my life is fated and that all human lives are fated to a certain degree. I was put into this circumstance. I have an obligation to tell the world what is happening on my ranch. Nobody was going to silence me.

After some time I left the woodshed, went back to the house at a sprint, grabbed a pair of binoculars that I keep in the house, and scanned the hillside across from the house to see if there was anybody still there. I knew that it was a sniper bullet that had gone through the walls. Anytime you get one shot from a high caliber gun like that it's a sniper. There was nothing that I could see in the hills. I called the Maricopa County Sheriff's Department. They came out and made a report. I answered all the usual questions.

Does anybody want harm upon you or your family?

Not that I know of.

Do you owe any money?

I paid cash for my ranch and I don't have any debts in the world right now.

Do you have any idea why someone might want to take a shot at you?

It was at this point that I decided to keep my mouth shut. What am I going to do? Tell one of Joe Arpaio's deputy sheriff's that I have become a voice in the world of UFOs and abductions and the paranormal and that the Men in Black came to my house and told me to stop talking publicly about it, and they walked right through the metal gate at the front of my laneway? There's only so much a normal person can take.

One of the most frustrating things about being in the exopolitics world is that it's a lot like having mystical experiences. There's very few people that you can share them with. They're not part of the normal human experience. Trying to share them with other people makes those people feel inadequate somehow. Every human being at some level, with very few exceptions, feels as though they are the center of the world. If they don't know something, then it's not worth knowing, and there's no way that the universe and all the powers that be would give these extraordinary experiences to someone else and not to them.

Everyone has a reality paradigm and their immediate conclusion is that you're crazy. It can't be that you're experiencing a transdimensional reality for which they have no consciousness. That would be a deficit or a deficiency in them. Therefore, it has to be you. You're off your medication. You're in the early stages of schizophrenia. You're in some form of mental imbalance caused by stress or trauma. Every encounter with the police and the silly and ridiculous line of questioning they give is so frustrating it almost equals the frustration of the events going on at the ranch themselves.

Some of you might ask, quite fairly, is the government really trying to suppress information about extraterrestrial incursions into our reality? I think it's best to answer this with an analogy.

There are three ranches like mine on a direct line north and south. The first is Skinwalker Ranch in Utah. The second is the Bradshaw Ranch in Sedona, Arizona. The final ranch is my ranch, Stardust ranch, the farthest south.

The Bradshaw Ranch is a curious location. It has had a good book written about it, *Merging Dimensions: The Opening Portals of Sedona.* It was bought by a Hollywood stuntman in 1945. He opened up a photography business. He also had a number of Hollywood movies shot on his land. Many of the old westerns from the fifties were shot at the Bradshaw Ranch in Arizona. The rolling red landscape and the cone like mountain structures made for excellent backdrops for the desolate western stories.

Bradshaw attracting Hollywood revitalized the entire area and there was a minor economy that flourished there. Now, here is what is curious about the Bradshaw Ranch. It *activated* in 1992. I use the word activate because there was no paranormal activity on this ranch until 1992. After 1992 the stories are outrageous. Many of them are similar to the kinds of stories you're reading in my book. However, the Bradshaw Ranch has things that are even weirder.

It is reported that raptors were seen walking around on the ranch. Here I mean the five or six foot dinosaur from millions of years ago. It is believed they came through a portal and left through the same portal. As ridiculous as this might sound, once the raptors disappeared, the footprints were photographed. The raptors were really there. Here is where I prove my thesis about the government.

In May of 2003 the government approached the son of the original Bradshaw. He had turned the location into a functioning cattle ranch. They told him they were buying the ranch. They gave their price. They told him that if he did not sell they would requisition the ranch under federal law. As you might well imagine, he sold the ranch. It is now run by the US Forestry service which keeps armed military men all around the perimeter. Anyone trying to walk up to the fence will be shot. Does that sound like a government interested in disclosing the phenomenon of magnetic fields, portals, and life from other dimensions? Believe me when I tell you, there is danger in going public with these stories.

The next incident at my ranch happened on a Friday night. Friday nights have always been the night for Joyce and I to go out and do something. Sometimes we went to visit friends in Glendale where we lived before we bought the ranch. Sometimes we went to Phoenix for a meal at a nice restaurant and to see a movie. Sometimes we went shopping. The point is that it was couple time. It was a time we had put aside in our rather busy and stressful week for us to be husband and wife and go and do something. I looked forward to Friday nights quite a bit as did Joyce.

On this particular Friday night, and I'm really trying to remember the timeline of my story here, but this would have been sometime around 2009-2010. When Joyce was finally ready, we went out the side door to where the truck was parked in the parking area of the ranch. As I was opening up the driver side door a loud crack commenced and we were under fire from what sounded to me like an AK-47. Of course, I know what an AK-47 sounds like because I owned AK-47s and I still own AK-47s. Joyce and I immediately took refuge at the front of the truck and we crouched down behind the engine block. Bullets whizzed all around us. The shots were coming once again from the other side of the highway up in the hills. I had my cell phone so I dialed the sheriff's department right away. We sat behind that truck for about fifteen minutes waiting for the sheriff to come. They came in full force. I guess some of my neighbors a little ways off called the sheriff's department as well, so there was no doubt on their part that there was an AK-47 being fired at us.

Again we went through the same line of questioning. Joyce and I were separated, as though this were some kind of a domestic dispute and they wanted to get two versions of the story. I understood, it's not that difficult to understand how cops think. It's standard procedure in therapy as well to separate people and to interview them separately. We told them everything we could tell them. What more was there to tell? We didn't know who was shooting at us. We didn't have any enemies that we knew of. We didn't owe any money. There was nobody making claim on our land. Nobody had come and made an offer on the land that we refused. Joyce didn't have an ex-husband. I didn't have a crazy ex-wife. We became something of a curiosity to Joe Arpaio's Maricopa County Sheriff Department.

At the lower levels of government, like a sheriff's office, they're not read in on the deeper secrets that the government at the federal level keep to themselves. They're just foot soldiers in the community trying to keep the peace. We had become a troubling breach of the peace, not by anything that we were doing, but by what was being done to us. So we had police cars in the neighborhood all the time after that. It made us feel safe from the human problems.

I do wonder sometimes how they keep the lie going. The Maricopa County Sheriff's Department must have had hundreds of calls about unidentified flying objects over the years. It would be impossible to be in law enforcement, receiving calls from the public, and not know that parts of Arizona were a hotspot for paranormal activity. Somehow the police always showed up and made it seem like there was nothing out of the ordinary and that your claim was profoundly unusual and that they had no corroboration from the neighborhood or from the county that anything that you were saying was even close to a public phenomenon. Another thing that surprises me is that community groups have not formed in Arizona as a result of all of the paranormal activity.

There is something about the experience of being abducted or the experience of seeing a disc close to your home that renders you mute. And here I mean mute to any kind of public conversation that might have a healing or understanding or expansion of knowledge and fact. It seems to me sometimes that one of the side effects of encountering extraterrestrials is that you isolate yourself. It's part of a general trend in human beings not to leave the herd. I put it squarely on the police for not beginning a dialogue with the public about all of the high strangeness that was happening in Rainbow Valley. In the end, though, when you give it a good think, all they are really commissioned to do is protect life and property. They have no role to explain things that are outside their job descriptions.

There was one time at the ranch where there was a giant black triangle hovering over Rainbow Valley. A blind man could have seen it. At that time, and this would have been around 2005-2006, I was still fairly secluded out there. So there were no neighbors out on the street gawking at the giant black triangle with me. I had Joyce call the Maricopa County Sheriff's Office. We told them exactly what was going on. They sent a car out with a single sheriff's deputy. He got out of the car and walked over toward me where I stood at the end of my laneway, by the iron gate where the Men in Black had walked right through. The deputy was wearing a rain jacket despite the fact that the sky was clear. He had a plastic wrap over his police hat. At first I thought maybe he was mentally retarded. It seemed that stupid to me what he was doing. Then it dawned on me. He had been told to come out and answer the call but not to identify himself.

The rain jacket and the plastic wrap over his hat were to cover up his badge number. He stood right in front of me communicating with dispatch through his walkie-talkie. He confirmed that he was at the location of my ranch, and he confirmed that there was in fact a giant black triangle hovering in the sky just above my ranch. It was as big as a football field. He told me there was nothing the sheriff's department could do to help me. I told him that I wanted an official report so that

I could have people understand what I was experiencing on the ranch was real. He looked at me and he said there would be no paperwork. And with that he turned and walked back to his cruiser, got in, and drove away. Again, I have to ask, what is the chain of command in these bizarre *X-Files* type events in the world of policing from the federal agencies like the FBI down to local sheriff's offices? Even standing on the street and watching one of the giant crafts with me, a Maricopa County Sheriff's Deputy was not willing to put on paper that he saw it.

The Big Man

There were parties that were interested in what was going on at my ranch. They just weren't public-sector. In the latter part of the first decade of the new millennium I heard from Robert Bigelow, chief executive officer a Bigelow Aerospace, at that time one of the largest private aerospace companies in the world.

Bigelow was known to have a fascination with space, extraterrestrials, and the paranormal. He was already scoping out the area before I bought Stardust Ranch, and he had bought Skinwalker Ranch. He gained a lot of fame through the stories that spread about paranormal activity very similar to what goes on at my ranch. He bought Skinwalker for $200,000 and sold it in 2016 for 4.5 million. The purchaser was a shell corporation nobody really knows anything about.

Now I want to be completely clear and upfront in this story. What is being presented are my ideas and opinions. If you want to consider me an expert for living on a paranormal, extraterrestrial infested, portal populated ranch in Rainbow Valley, Arizona, then yes, at an experiential level, you could probably call me an expert, but you don't live through what I've lived through and not begin to research what's going on. My disposition towards everything that's been going on around me has never been fear, rather an innate curiosity to get to the bottom of it. I try to see the phenomenon as rationally as possible, so to understand the UFOs I did as much research as I could, and most of it was first hand. I reached out and contacted experts, experiencers, and abductees in the field. As already stated in this story, most of the people were doing late-night radio like Coast-to-Coast or publishing small websites. The community wasn't really that strong.

Things really got interesting when Bigelow's people reached out to me. It's hard to say what's going on with a guy like Bigelow. My knee-jerk, or my intuition, is that he's a cooperating assistant to the government forces trying to cover up the UFO and paranormal phenomenon. Why do I say this? It's just based on observing his behavior. He's really done nothing to increase the public's awareness about the phenomenon going on at these ranches, other than hokey horror films and cryptic documentaries. Consider this as well, Bradshaw Ranch was forcibly taken by the government. Why would they allow a civilian to own Skinwalker Ranch, a civilian who owns am aerospace company, and a civilian who is a billionaire? He's contributed nothing to a furtherance of our understanding of the world and the dimensions that we live within. Bigelow is with the shady agencies and departments that cover up what's going on.

Their *Who We Are* section of their website reads as follows.

Entrepreneur Robert T. Bigelow is the Founder and President of Bigelow Aerospace, LLC. Headquartered in Las Vegas, Nevada, Bigelow Aerospace is a general contracting, research and development company that concentrates on achieving economic breakthroughs in the costs associated with the design, development, and construction of habitable space structures for private enterprise and government use. Since 1999, Mr. Bigelow has personally provided all financial support totaling over $350 million to date. In addition, Mr. Bigelow provides the daily strategic leadership at Bigelow Aerospace in its design, development, and testing of expandable habitat architectures where Bigelow Aerospace employs approximately 150 employees at its Las Vegas facility. Mr. Bigelow has successfully launched two subscale spacecraft called Genesis I & II into orbit as well as the Bigelow Expandable Activity Module (BEAM), which is attached to the Tranquility module of the International Space Station. Moreover, Mr. Bigelow serves as the program manager of the B330 spacecraft – Bigelow Aerospace's main habitation system for LEO and beyond LEO destinations.

Robert Bigelow is an experienced general contractor, designer, developer, financier, buyer and manager of many large real estate projects in the US. Mr. Bigelow holds the exclusive licensing rights to commercialize expandable habitat technology originally conceived but abandoned by NASA in the 1990's. Over the last seventeen years, Mr. Bigelow has earned over twenty patents, launched three prototype spacecraft, partnered with NASA on several contracts, built the necessary facilities to design and fabricate expandable habitat technology, and has advocated for a sustainable commercial space economy.[1]

So why is this guy the sole private entrepreneur buying transdimensional ranches? Who knows for sure? Anyway, Big Daddy Bigelow took an interest in my ranch.

The first group to reach out was a group associated with John Lear. He's from the Lear Jet family. He's an ex fighter pilot and big voice in the exopolitics community. He was also very negative toward me. He believed I was making everything up and that I was just trying to get attention. And they were very nasty about it. They called up on the phone and told me I was lying. I guess I had reached a point in my journey where the world proper had to deal with me. Believe it or not, this world of extraterrestrials and UFOs is populated by a bunch of huge egos, just like the book publishing industry, Hollywood, or big business. People who have made their names in this world are very aggressive and very domineering when it comes to protecting their territory. And as I have said already in my story, so many of them have connections to the military and the intelligence communities that you really have to wonder what's going on. Lear is another example of one of these goofballs who's half in and half out of the intelligence agencies. Remember, there's an old saying, once you're in the CIA you're always in the CIA until you die. There is no retirement from the intelligence community. So I trusted John Lear about as far as I can throw him.

I'm out there on Internet radio and on chat boards and on UFO sites like Peter Gersten's and I'm talking about all of this phenomenon, so sooner or later I had to be dealt with. I was like a kid banging two trash can lids together at three o'clock in the morning on a suburban cul-de-sac. One of the neighbors is going to come out or the police are going to show up sooner or later. John Lear and his people ended up leading me to Bigelow. He called me up and said, You want to sell the ranch?

I told him I'd love to sell the ranch.

---

[1]https://bigelowaerospace.com/pages/whoweare/

He asked me how much I wanted.

I told him.

He made an offer.

The offer was far less than sufficient.

This bantering about price in buying the ranch went on for about six months to a year. And then one day Bigelow called me up and said he'd like to send a team of people out to investigate the ranch, and he said that if my claims were true he would buy the ranch. We agreed to these terms.

Bigelow dispatched a team from Las Vegas, the headquarters of Bigelow Aerospace. On the appointed day I waited but nobody showed up. I got a call from Bigelow's people from Las Vegas. The vehicles he sent got as far as the bridge crossing over into Rainbow Valley and they broke down — all of them. Bigelow's people told me that they would have to reschedule and that the vehicles in Rainbow Valley would have to be towed back to Las Vegas.

I didn't know what to make of their story. I half believed it and half disbelieved it. However, Given my own history at the ranch and the surrounding area it was entirely plausible that all of their new vehicles broke down at the same spot at the same time. Nonetheless, one week later I was contacted and they wanted to send another team. I agreed but told them that if anything happened all expense and liability was on their side, not mine. They agreed. A week later later the appointed team showed up. They came into the house and did interviews with Joyce and I. They asked a bunch of questions. They recorded the interviews on video. We were both given digital lie detector tests.

They asked me to reenact everything related to the killing of the first gray in the sunroom. I did. They stayed for two or three days and continued to ask questions. They didn't live with us at the ranch, They had a hotel close by. They went around the property doing tests with some kind of electronic instrumentation. They took hundreds of pictures.

After about a week they left. I was promised a formal written report by Bigelow Aerospace. No such report was forthcoming. After about a week Bob Bigelow started calling. He wanted to buy the ranch, but his price was half of what we agreed upon to allow his team onto my land to do their tests. So he changed the purchase price and he reneged on his word to give me a copy of the report. Bob Bigelow is a scumbag.

I've continued to hear from Bob over the years. Time and time again he calls me up and makes an offer on the ranch but it's too low. It's been going on for years. The funny thing is Bigelow has not published a lot of information in the public space about his research. The one thing that bothers me the most about Bigelow and his company, Bigelow Aerospace, is that they are as secretive and non-cooperative as the government when it comes to this fourth dimension stuff, hence my aforementioned opinion on aerospace billionaires and the government.

One of the more curious things that resulted from Bigelow's team going over the ranch is the theory that there is a UFO craft buried underneath the ranch. At the time that Bigelow sent his team out, he also made a request to excavate the ranch. I told them there was no way I would allow that unless he bought the ranch. Over the years I've received numerous claims from various people, including airline pilots, psychics, and other people who just call me up to tell me there is a pulse coming from my ranch.

The Bigelow team made one more visit to the ranch, two in total. They took samples from the walls using a special light that pinpoints human blood. They were interested in tissue samples. In the time I had been living at the ranch I had killed numerous grays. A number of them with my samurai sword, and a number of them with my bare hands, picking them up by the ankles and just smashing them into walls. And so there was gray fluid all over the place. I didn't have any bodies for them. The bodies kept disappearing out of my freezer. How that happened, you might ask? Probably the same way my car keys would disappear and then drop on top of my head a couple days later. What do you want me to say? Things are phasing in and out of the reality of my home. But they weren't able to clean up the tissue samples. Bigelow did call back and did say that he was interested in buying the ranch. He did not offer me the price that we had agreed upon if his tests were verified. He confirmed that the tests returned results that were commensurate with the phenomenon I was describing. I will give him that. What he did not give me was an actual paper copy of the report done by his team. And for that I call Bob Bigelow a liar. He continues to call from time to time making inquiries about the ranch and still pitching me a lowball offer.

Chapter 15

Smoking Gun

After sometime, we received word back from Dr. Levengood. The sample I had sent by FedEx had been analyzed.

Blood

The sample appears to be pure hemoglobin like that found at the Cattle Mutilation sites with what appears to be segment rods in the blood, never seen anything like it.

Skin

Looks like segmented grass except it's not grass.

Levengood proved to be an odd person to interact with, but then again, who isn't in the UFO world? In the beginning, after the introduction facilitated by Captain Robert Collins, he was very excited to receive my materials. There was somewhat regular correspondence by email. I was kept in the loop with everything that was going on. I had increased my public presence through the Internet and through alternative radio shows like Coast-to-Coast. The presence of the grays continued. There were regular attempted abductions. The marks on my body and Joyce's body continued. I occasionally had an animal destroyed. But over the years it was so intermittent it isn't worth calling a regular occurrence. Another person I met during this time, introduced to me by Captain Robert Collins, was a man named Derrel Sims.

Sims billed himself and still does as *The UFO Hunter*. I know, you can't make this stuff up. The world of exopolitics is more bizarre than the freak alley in the old Barnum Bailey Circus. He still maintains an active presence in the UFO world through a website called Alien Hunter.

Think you've had alien contact? Are you puzzled by unusual physical marks, missing time, strange Dreams, or even X-rays that your doctor doesn't understand? If any of this is keeping you up at night, then maybe it's time you called...

Derrel Sims, The Alien Hunter. The world's leading expert on alien abductions. His 38+ years of field research has focused on physical evidence, and led to his groundbreaking discoveries of alien implants and alien fluorescence. As a former military police officer and CIA operative, Sims has a unique insight to the alien organization which he believes functions similarly to an intelligence agency.

Sims is also a compassionate and skilled therapist and Certified Master Hypnotherapist who has helped hundreds of alien experiencers all over the world come to terms with what they've witnessed...

Like so many people in the UFO world, you have to ask yourself where Sims is coming from. Time and time again you are greeted by a half in and half out person — people with former intelligence or military intelligence connections, retired, or as close as one can be to retired when you come from that world. They seem to be the dominant genus in the exopolitics world, and there's not one of them who is telling everything they know. The one exception that comes to mind is the ex-Canadian Defense Minister, Paul Hellyer. He is a grand statesman of the exopolitics world and the highest ranking government official in a NATO country to go public with the UFO phenomenon.

The rest of the crew, the Americans, are an assortment of people with mixed motivations, and many times I wonder if they're really in the UFO space to help people understand what's really going on or to continue a kind of cover-up of what's really going on. Perhaps I'm being a little tough on them. There is also the case of the person who wants to do the right thing but they are constrained by a non-disclosure agreement that they signed while they were in the military or the intelligence world. At this time, and this was the later years of the first decade of the new millennium, Sims was all over my tissue sample story. He was liaising with Dr. Levengood as closely as I was. We were all anxiously awaiting the results.

The last correspondence I had with Levengood had him stating the following:

You have the smoking gun. This is proof of alien life visiting Earth and links the phenomenon together positively!

All of my actions as it regarded the disclosure of what was going on at the ranch, including the physical evidence that could prove my claims, and the investigation by Bigelow's people, most of them former FBI and CIA, and all the other evidence I had gathered over the years I had been living on the ranch, were accumulating to a *prima facie* case that the extraterrestrial presence on earth is real. To some people, I might sound a little paranoid, a little underwhelmed in the manner I went about disclosing what was going on at my ranch, but you have to realize it had been years of strange visitations at the ranch, both off-world visitations and strange, cryptic, deceitful human visitations.

I told Levengood I wanted to be in control of all press releases related to the sample results. By the end of June 2011, after a couple of years of dealing with Levengood in the lab, he told me in phone conversations that he might never write a formal report, adding that he was very excited about the samples, which contained tiny segmented fibers that were not cloth. Levengood explained that blood does not contain segmented fibers. This made my sample highly unusual. He also explained that normal antibodies that are positive or negative determine the type of blood. The samples I gave him were something totally different. He called it a very peculiar case because the cell parts looked like joint grass but were not grass. When I asked him why he didn't send the tissue out for DNA testing, he said there wasn't enough material and it was very expensive.

I believe Levengood was threatened. In every step of my journey there has been some shadow I cannot see. The most direct manifestation of it was the Men in Black floating through my gate and walking down my laneway, and of course there were the shots taken at me. All the time I was dogged by the shadow. I often wondered why they didn't just kill me. Maybe they had calculated that doing that would make my story explode, create a kind of UFO martyr out of me that would garner more attention than they wanted. I really can't answer any questions that pertain to the force that was working against me in my attempt to make the world know that my ranch was having alien visitations.

Sims tried his best to get Levengood back on track. He even went out to Michigan to make a personal visit. It was then that I heard through Sims that Dr. Levengood had died. He was quite elderly at the time. His death was extremely understandable. However I couldn't shake the feeling that this was just another bizarre occurrence in what had been a decade and a half of bizarre occurrences for me at the ranch. I might also add at this juncture, for those who think I am being a bit paranoid, the Skinwalker Ranch was bought by Bigelow, who in my estimation is in cahoots with the government in terms of the see nothing-hear nothing approach to UFO disclosure, and the Bradshaw Ranch was literally requisitioned by the federal government and taken over with a perimeter fence all around it and armed guards.

I was the last of the three desert hot spots in a direct line from Utah down to Rainbow Valley, and I was the only one still in private hands and looking to disclose publicly what was going on. So if I sound paranoid to you, remember that you have not walked a single step in my shoes. You have not dealt with the kinds of people in the exopolitics world. You have not dealt with the government. You have not dealt with the gray aliens, and you have not dealt with the Men in Black.

I didn't give up with Sims. The UFO world is full of people who want to be the ones who prove that aliens are real. I sometimes wonder, though, if that is real. I sometimes get the impression that people just like to live in a reality where they believe in UFOs. Or maybe I'm being too hard on these people and myself. There is a tremendous human need to be part of the group. Government knows this very well. In the absence of government support in the UFO world, the collection of unorganized human beings are left to their own, and it becomes a kind of premodern anthropological experiment.

Human beings do not organize well. As much as the hippie types want to believe that we can live without authority and centralized leadership, in my experience it's very difficult. Most communal forms of living not centered on a strict religious code, whether it be an ashram in India or Mennonites in the United States, fall apart. And the UFO world is no exception. There is more backstabbing, Roman-style politics, and high drama than a Colombian soap opera.

It's like a microcosm of everything that's wrong with the human race. This is unfortunate. UFO visitation and contact with the human race is, in my opinion, the most important event in human history aside from the visitations from spiritual persons who come to teach us, and in many cases, even these people may have extraterrestrial connections. Unless stars can move on their own, the star of Bethlehem that appeared when Christ was born was a UFO.

The main problem in the UFO world is the jockeying for position as an authority, and the various classifications of people. It runs the gamut. You have academics who do very good work like Rich Dolan and John Mack, PhD level research and organization into a competent and well sourced presentation. The academics are well-liked in the UFO world but they burn their reputations in the normal academic world, making themselves laughingstocks.

Just look at what they did to John Mack. He was six months buried and his work at Harvard was overturned by the young upstart Susan Clancy who returned abduction to the field of human repressed memory of childhood trauma, completely negating the reality of the experience and relegating it to the world of psychiatry and a non-functioning brain that cannot allow the human consciousness to experience the full childhood trauma in adulthood. So not too many academics come into the UFO world. I should be clear and point out here that when I say UFO world I mean the world presented by unorganized human beings who are not getting paid.

Another class of person in the UFO world is the contactee. A contact is somebody who is contacted by a benign UFO race, and by benign I mean a race that doesn't want to eat or kill us. They are viewed with fascination but tremendous skepticism. Another group of people are the abductees. These are people who are taken involuntarily by a hostile alien race who do not respect human autonomy. The final class of people in the UFO World are our clandestine government people. The government loves to plant people in the UFO world. There is more disinformation spread about UFOs by the government than any other kind of information coming into the UFO world.

The largest and most successful organization in the UFO world is MUFON, which stands for Mutual UFO Network. They bill themselves as follows:

MUFON is an all-volunteer, non-profit 501(c)3 charitable corporation and the world's oldest and largest civilian UFO investigation & research organization. Our goal is to be the inquisitive minds' refuge seeking answers to that most ancient question, "Are we alone in the universe?" The answer very simply, is NO. Whether you have UFO reports to share, armchair UFO investigator aspirations, or want to train and join our investigation team, MUFON is here for you. Won't you please join us in our quest to discover the truth?

Because these groups are organized by volunteers, they always have money problems. Such is the case with MUFON. They went through an experience in which Robert Bigelow tried to take them over by influencing the organization with money. If it were not for the threat of resignation from the senior people who had been at MUFON for years, Bigelow would be running it today. Based on my experiences with him, I do not think that would be a step forward for the UFO world.

Dr. Levengood died before we could sort out going public with the tissue sample. Nobody in his organization, which was only a half dozen people or so, took over his initiative. I didn't have the money to send the sample to a DNA lab, so the dead alien remains an unaccepted reality in the larger UFO world.

Where's the Proof

I can hear you thinking. I know what you're thinking because I have the same thoughts. In the UFO world the experiencers live in two worlds. One world is the world of experience. We experience things that normal people do not. I apologize for using the word normal. There is no normal in the human experience. I need to use a word that creates two groups. Forgive me for calling non-UFO experiencers normal. I use the word because it is the common world, the world of living your life, the world of reading newspapers in North America and Western Europe, the world of watching our news programs, documentaries, reading books, the world we share by common means. This is the common human experience.

From this common human experience you're thinking: why didn't you call the government with your tissue sample; why didn't you send samples to more than one lab; why didn't you call newspapers; why did you wait so long to send a sample out; and do you really expect me to believe that after all of this Dr. Levengood just didn't care anymore?

The simple answer is no. I'm not asking you to believe anything. I am telling you the way things happened. I am also telling you that there are reasons why things happen a certain way in the world of exopolitics. It is one of the most surveilled, controlled, and feared groups on the planet. The exopolitics community, especially in the United States, has been for decades watched more closely than any terrorist cell in the world. Why?

Why do things disappear in the UFO World? Why do people suddenly get cold feet about going forward with earth shattering news? Why does evidence go missing? Why did a drunk driver drive up onto a sidewalk to run over John Mack while giving a lecture in London? Why do the abductees have their memories wiped? Why would the next academic at Harvard to publish on abductions after John Mack completely and utterly contradict his work? Why have so many of us met these Men in Black? Yes, it's true. It's not just me who met the Men in Black, Many of the people I have interacted with have also met the Men in Black. I stood up to them. I don't have the fear gene. I'm stupid that way. My wife Joyce has been harmed in horrible ways because of the decisions I've made. I have to live with that. People in the UFO world have been murdered or silenced with threats against their family.

I can hear you thinking. You think we live in a world that is run fairly. You think we live in a world with full disclosure. You have been conditioned to think that way. You have been mentally controlled to think that way. Your entire life is a drama put on for you by people who get paid to do it. The disparity at present between what our governments know and what the general population knows is so great we are like two different species. The general public is neanderthal man. The government insiders are the homosapien.

It's a dangerous place for us to be. The neanderthals did not fare well. Even the way I speak to you is compromised. I have no choice. The metaphor I used is factually incorrect in the non-normal world I live in. In the world I now live in, human beings were seeded on this planet. Evolution is part of the fairy tale that has been told to you. So in using the metaphor of neanderthal man and homosapien I am bridging the normal world and the world I have been pulled into through my experiences at Stardust Ranch. The gap between the world and the transgovernmental insiders is so great now that we run the risk of being wiped out and having them start a new version of humanity.

Now I can hear some of you thinking I'm paranoid once again. What kind of a group of human beings would wipe out billions of people to start a new civilization based on science that only they know, given to them from extraterrestrials, and not shared with the rest of the world? The answer is any kind of people. If you look at the history of the human race, the history that is somewhat true, most of our research and advancement has come from military inventions, or from inventions that came out of military funding.

The moment one country, people, or region of the world, surpasses another part of the world in any tactical way, the result is always the same. The tactically superior humans decimate the tactically inferior humans. The superiors take over the land and the resources of the inferiors and very few of the inferiors are left living. This is what we did to the natives in North, South, and Central America. They survive in Central and South America in healthy numbers because the Spanish conquistadors had difficulty chasing them through the mountainous jungle areas. It wasn't the easy kill of the North American Indians on open desert areas like Arizona and long flat planes like the prairies in Canada.

We pretend to be sorry about it now, centuries after the fact, but it's still a complete lie. We don't do anything to really help the native populations. Our position is assimilate or die. It's not just a technological superiority that produces these results. Muhammad did the same thing with the Quran. This was the new consciousness technology in that region of the world and those who did not comply died by the sword. The same thing with the Gospels.

The Vatican was the backbone of all European exploration. It could not have happened without the support of the Vatican. You never hear that where they went, the consciousness technology of Christianity, which the Europeans viewed as superior, was meant to replace the indigenous way of thinking and believing. Of course the natives did a lot more than believe. They were experiencers of the transdimensional reality that human beings live in because they had not been conditioned by a rigorous school system that commences at the age of five and an indoctrination process to wipe out the imagination, and they had been led to plant based consciousness separators like ayahuasca, peyote, and mushrooms.

I think you understand what I'm trying to say. The sudden expansion of consciousness does not always produce a loving person. The example of the highly evolved human beings who have come into this drama on planet earth to try and teach us is not the norm. The normal result of a sudden expansion of consciousness, and the influx of extraterrestrial contact and technology at the government level since World War II has been a sudden expansion of consciousness, usually results in the new superman killing the old normal man. This is where we are now in the early twenty-first century. It's one of the most dangerous places we have ever been as a species. We have to try to understand what is happening on our planet. It's a matter of life and death.

Chapter 16

Visitors

If you've stayed with me so far in the story, I feel the need at this point to say — it gets weird.

Sometime around the third week in July 2011 I received a phone call. If you've been listening to the story, you know a lot of people call me out of the blue. People who think they've been touched by God, people who think they spoken to aliens themselves, people who believe themselves to be powerful clairvoyants or psychics — and many really are gifted seers — and just regular people who have heard about my story through the play it had gotten in the exopolitics arena. By this time I had been out in the world almost a decade. Remember, when I started this story I told you the most difficult part for me would be the timeline. I've been on this ranch since June 1st 1996.

A lot of the things that I described in the early part of the book just kept repeating themselves. I didn't want to stress that too much. We were getting to this. But the abductions were quite consistent. The markings on my body were quite consistent and, to be clear, I killed a lot of grays. I hated the little bastards. It was an acute sense of territory and defense of home and family, but that might be making excuses for myself. I don't have a lot of regrets about killing the grays. I don't kill them anymore. I made my peace with the grays, or I was allowed to make my peace with the grays. Let me put it this way, within all of us is a simple animal consciousness.

Sufism talks about seven souls: mineral, vegetable, animal, personal, human, and secret souls, and the secret of secrets. We all have an animal inside of us. Put your hand into a gopher hole sometime and see if you don't get bit, same thing for a badger. Walk into a den of wolves and see what happens, a cave with a jaguar in it. Of course, I'm not really recommending you go out and do these things. I am of course just demonstrating the law of the home. Defending the home is a spiritual law to my sensibilities. Even insects have it. Go and kick around a big ant hill sometime. See if the ants don't bite you. So I'm not apologizing for killing the grays. I am however saying that it was an expression of my animal soul, in the Sufi sense.

The person who called me in mid-July of 2011 was a new kind of weird. She introduced herself as Doctor Brandy Howe. She told me that a third-party had hired her to come out to my ranch and see if she could help me. She did not at that time say who the third party was. We talked for about five minutes. I gave anybody who called me a serious ear for at least five minutes. That's all the time I need to weed out the cranks. She called herself a doctor because she healed people and animals. She seemed to me the embodiment of everything that Arizona had come to represent in the flaky New Age world. It's probably best to let her website speak for her. It's called Nite Star Life Awareness, and the landing page has the following introduction.

Brandy L. Howe, DD, Traditional Naturopath, Life Science Practitioner, has over 30 years experience in the study of Alternative/Integrative healing. In March, 1996, she received her Doctor of Naturopathy degree with High Honors through the Clayton School of Natural Healing. In February, 2002, she attained Doctor of Divinity and is an ordained minister. She is a Reiki Master/Teacher, Animal Intuitive Lightworker, Electromagnetic Practitioner, Certified Organic Consultant and a Licensed Facilitator for Joyful Child, Inc.

Dr. Howe's studies include herbology, pharmacology, nutrition, aromatherapy, iridology, homeopathy, polarity therapy, acupressure, kinesiology, reflexology, healing, vibrational therapies and remedies, animal communication, spiritual/intuitive guidance and bereavement assistance.

We set a date for July 31st, 2011.

Cynthia Crawford

The most curious thing about Brandy's call was who paid her. It was a woman by the name of Cynthia T Crawford. In a world of strange tales, and the world of extraterrestrials is certainly a world of strange tales, Miss Crawford's is in the top one percent.

She was born a fraternal twin. but she had a different blood and tissue type than her twin sister, and, unlike her twin sister, she was born without an amniotic sac. According to medical history, this is the first time that this has ever happened. It left the doctors more than a little bit confused, but that was not the first time that Cynthia Crawford would baffle and confuse people. It was in fact just the beginning of a lifetime of bafflement.

To tell Cynthia's story we have to go to the very root of the *modern* exopolitics world. It begins in World War II. This is not to say that extraterrestrials have not been on this planet longer than that; they most certainly have, and they have influenced almost every aspect of human expression, but that's a story for a later chapter. Cynthia's father was a member of the OSS — the Office of Strategic Services — the progenitor of the CIA. Our engagement with the Nazis is part of an untold story in world history. It's broken out in the world of UFO lore, but that doesn't mean it has mainstream acceptance. Much like Dr. John Mack trying to bring abductions to the world, mainstream academe has done very little to introduce the idea of extraterrestrials commingling and participating with the human race in major historical events. This is where researchers like Richard Dolan play such a strong role. His work on the exoteric aspect of the exopolitical world has been astounding, a breath of fresh air in an otherwise unprofessional and unstandardized world.

The Nazis were so far ahead of the rest of the world technologically that they were even creating UFOs. They didn't dream these things up on their own. They had help from extraterrestrials. The story told by William Tompkins, a retired aviation executive and extraterrestrial familiar his whole life, affirms that the Nazi Party made an alliance with a group of Draco Reptilians, of the Draco star system. These are the reptilians that David Icke was laughed out of polite society for talking about in the mid-nineties with his breakout book, *The Biggest Secret*. Icke is telling the truth. The Draco Reptilians have played a huge role in human history for millennia. They are so integrated into human culture that we can hardly tell what's theirs and what's ours anymore, especially at the level of religions. We'll get more into the reptilians in a subsequent chapter.

Undoubtedly, Crawford's father was privy to a lot of the early UFO secrets when the Nazis folded up and went to Antarctica. They didn't actually lose the war. The Nazi Party is alive and well. The people they left behind were part of a distribution plan between Russia and the United States called *Project Paperclip*, which is actually referenced by name in the Hollywood movie, *Captain America: The Winter Soldier*. Remember, it's been the military-industrial-entertainment complex for some time. The cutting-edge science of the Nazi Party was distributed between the two ruling political systems in the world, communism and capitalism.

This was the beginning of the breakaway civilization I discussed in the previous chapter. The knowledge and science inherited from the Nazi Party was so overwhelming that secret divisions of an as of yet unnamed intelligence agency were created. The OSS became the CIA in 1947, with parts of the OSS continuing on autonomously for some time afterwards, but the bulk of intelligence went to the CIA.

Cynthia's father was approached by officers of the OSS to be part of a very secret government project. He signed back up with the army to work for the project with the OSS, a project so secret that Cynthia herself was not told until her mid-thirties. Her father then told her that she was a hybrid human being created in an OSS program with deoxyribonucleic acid from two different alien races combined with human DNA.

Now most people when they hear this kind of information immediately jump to a bad and evil government position. This is the basis of an entire culture of conspiracy theory which has evolved in the last few decades, especially spiking after September 11th, 2001, and becoming a louder and louder voice not only in America but in other parts of the world as well. As I said earlier in my story, the human race has a collective unconscious, and they can be lied to for only so long before something very disturbing starts to dominate their consciousness. It doesn't mean that they have all the answers. They can't go to court and make a case against the government, but at a very fundamental level everybody knows that they're being lied to now.

Hollywood has received a lot of its ideas from the intelligence world, and this is not just a question of keeping the public informed. The intelligence world knows what I'm telling you. They know we live within a collective consciousness. By letting the information out under the classification of fiction they are able to release some of the pressure building up in the human unconscious. It is, as described in the earlier chapter, a false catharsis, an extraction of all of the negative and toxic emotions that are building up in human consciousness through a two-dimensional picture projected onto a movie screen.

They also started up the mind control and mind strengthening programs that fall under the umbrella of MK Ultra. These were begun with the CIA through the satellite office that operated out of McGill Hospital University in Montreal, Canada. All of this is verifiable. The Canadian authorities have gone through class action suits by the survivors of the original programs. My point in bringing all of this up is that we saw something in World War II through our engagement with the Nazis that changed the way we think about our reality forever. The only problem is that experience was not universal for the whole human race. Had it been universal, we might be living in a very different society now, one humbled by the reality that we were not alone in this solar system, the Milky Way Galaxy, or the trillions of galaxies that exist.

So much changed in World War II that an entire history has to be written for the last seventy-five years. The history we have now is pretty much entirely a lie except for certain spot on dates like the bombing of Dresden or the bombing of London. The motivations for that war and the forces at play in that war have never been revealed to the human race. Nor has it been revealed that we did not win World War II. It just sort of ended when the Nazi establishment went to Antarctica. You could say that the modern exopolitical world begins with what was harvested from the Nazis through Project Paperclip. The first questions that we could ask about Miss Crawford are where did the OSS come up with two different types of alien DNA, and why was the OSS, which was tasked with intelligence during World War II, the holder of alien DNA at the end of World War II?

All of these are questions I can't answer. I'm only bringing these things into my story to help you understand the UFO phenomenon and, at a certain point in this story, we're going to hit the crossroads; we're going to hit the point of this story, and you need to understand these details, and you need to understand when the actual exopolitical reality became such a focus of the intelligence communities in the world.

As a toddler, Cynthia was routinely visiting medical facilities that were run clandestinely underground by the military. She went through a battery of examinations. She would later recall a host of alien abductions, examinations, impregnations, as well as miraculous healings and organ replacements. For the fifties and into the seventies, she desperately tried to understand her experiences, but there was nothing similar being talked about in public back then. It's sometimes difficult for us in the first quarter of the new millennium to imagine a world without the Internet and any question we have being reasonably answered in a matter of seconds, but that was life back then.

It must have been hard for her to go through her ordeal alone, factoring in as well her need to talk about these things and how these things would be greeted by the uninitiated. She was very often viewed as completely insane. She had psychic abilities. It wasn't until she faced these otherworldly beings that she transcended her fear, and it was then that she learned that they were in fact her family. From that she awakened to her mission and why she had been brought to this planet in the first place. Confused yet? What do you think that last part means, *why she came to this planet?* What came to the planet? She was born of three different kinds of DNA mixed together, two alien and one human part. But she claims that she came to this planet. This is an important point in the alien narrative, and it also is a point at which the story gets very esoteric.

Deoxyribonucleic acid has to be in frequency with the astral form that it is going to incarnate into it. Now I need you to stop here for a moment. So many things in our religious and spiritual traditions can be explained with the addition of the alien narrative and what it has taught us. When the Vedic, Buddhist, Sikh teachers and others tell us that karma is infallible and that nobody can escape the consequences of their actions or the benefits, they are referring to this relationship between DNA and frequency. A frequency is a composition of thoughts and feelings. There's probably a much better word than frequency but I can't think of it.

No matter how comfortable a dark human being seems to be with their actions, a mafia enforcer, a vicious police officer, a corrupt politician, and anyone else you can think of, a part of them is recording everything, and a part of them is not in concert with what they are doing. The true nature of all sentient beings is to give. But this has to be learned over time through incarnations. Each and every time we live a life where we become very self-centered and damaging to the people around us, there's a sleeping part of us that knows everything that we're doing and records it, and when we die we are reminded of it. When we incarnate we seek an incarnation that will rectify the imbalance. We seek atonement. There are no dark forces controlling us on the other side, at least not as it pertains to the original construction of the creator.

We judge ourselves. This is why forgiveness is such an important part of spiritual traditions. You are literally saying you do not want to be part of a karmic cycle that is going to draw you back into circumstances in the future. You are willing to absorb the pain and the injustice that has been done to you, which might well be the result of an injustice you did in a past life, and you are willing to move on. For the greater good you forgive. And according to Cynthia, she came to earth on a mission of greater good. She came here on a spiritual mission. To fulfill that mission she had to go through all kinds of mental and physical suffering. She chose to do all of that. So the alien DNA was to bring her in as a spiritual being, to bring an alien vibration into a human atmosphere. It couldn't be done any other way. Now stop and think for a moment about Christ. His frequency was angelic if his father was the Archangel Gabriel.

I don't recall meeting Cynthia, but I did. It might have been in the early two thousands at some kind of UFO Meetup. I had started making the rounds in the new millennium, and my story was well known. But I had not spoken with Cynthia for any number of years, so long in fact that I didn't recall meeting her when I was first told it was she who paid for Dr. Brandy Howe to come to my ranch to try and aid me.

It wasn't until many years later, 2017 to be exact, that I would see Cynthia Crawford again. She came out to the ranch to visit me. She had three large tumors in her brain. She knew she was going to die. I was one of the last people that she would see before she left this world. She died a couple days after visiting me at the ranch. I am eternally grateful to this day for what she did for me. It was such a comfort to meet her, to have someone understand what I had been going through at the ranch, and to better understand myself, and why I'd gone through all the experiences I had. We choose our lives. We sign up for them before we are born. A friend of mine once told me that on the other side history is written from the future backwards. In the Sufi cosmology there should be a galactic soul, a way of describing oneself as a being that has life in the universe, not just the earth. Perhaps they lacked the language. Cynthia was a galactic soul. Her consciousness had memory and knowledge of herself as a galactic being. She made it abundantly clear to me my mission was to tell the world what was going on at my ranch. It was time they knew. I am fulfilling that promise to her and myself.

Chapter 17

July 31 2011

Cynthia Crawford had told Brandy that I was being attacked by a band of renegade gray aliens. I had no idea that renegades existed in extraterrestrial cultures. You live and you learn. Brandy had been abducted since the age of four, and these experiences had formed the adult who could do what she did, which was confront negative extraterrestrials. I suppose you could compare it to an exorcism, but, instead of demonic forces, extraterrestrials had to be removed. She did not come from a military family, which I found both surprising and refreshing. Many of the abductions are associated with families that are in the military. This may suggest that the family member in the military has entered into an agreement and given consent to allow their children to be abducted and trained by alien races.

This was certainly the case with Cynthia Crawford with a father in the CIA progenitor the OSS. It's another chapter in the undocumented and largely unknown world of government involvement in the UFO culture which is just now beginning to enter the human dialogue. According to Brandy, she was told to go out to the ranch with two warriors from Sirius, and that would be the constellation Sirius. She referred to them only as Jay and Jay, kind of like the two brothers from the old Bob Newhart show, those these Jays were not brothers. It was at this point that I learned that Sirius was a warrior culture that was aligned with a *Galactic Council* and used for enforcement of the laws that govern said council. As Brandy put it, *if you need something done, get some Sirians.*

According to what Brandy told me, as they were driving up the

154

road toward my ranch gate, somebody in the car noticed four clouds and pointed them out to the other passengers. They were very odd formations. Brandy looked up and told them they were not clouds; they were ships. She explained that very often alien ships mask themselves as clouds, but if you have the eyes to see, the formations will let you know they are ships. And sure enough, the moment she recognized them as ships, they uncloaked. Everybody in the car saw them for a moment before they cloaked back again. This was the backup. Brandy was told telepathically that five ships had been sent to support her mission at the ranch.

A short distance before they arrived at the ranch, Brandy felt a presence off to her right and she told the Jays there was an underground hub for the grays there. It was putting out a vibration she could feel. By hub, she meant a place where the gray aliens congregated. When they arrived at the ranch and got out of the vehicle, Brandy felt a magnificent energy. This is the duality of Stardust Ranch. Even with all the negativity, the animal slaughters, the levitating wife, the abductions, and the sorted litany of dirty deeds, my ranch could imbue you with a strangely reverent feeling, even holy, I dare say, despite the grays and their negativity.

Brandy also felt the presence of those who were, as she describes it, *not of the light*, a one size fits all term for entities and beings of a dark, self-serving nature. Brandy told me in our initial conversation she believed the reason the gray aliens had settled at my ranch was because they were attracted to the higher vibration energy. I found that a bit odd. I really didn't understand it at the time. Why would negative beings be attracted to a positive energy? I would later in my sojourn at the ranch realize that the world was not so black and white as I had conceived it to be. There were far more nuances. Positive energy is constructive.

Everything needs positive energy. It is the essence of the creator, and all things, good and bad, need it. It was an important realization for me. It helped me find forgiveness and understanding on the ranch, and that was the beginning of a great healing. I had been so dualistic in my thinking and actions. I had been throwing gasoline on the fire, killing the gray aliens when I could, hating them, feeding them. It was an energy seepage that was like a nectar to them, like honey for a bear.

The Suicide

I went out of the house and greeted Brandy and her companions. Joyce was supposed to be there but she was late. I told them she would be joining us later. I noticed they had brought swords, and here I mean medieval broadswords, real swords, so real in fact I wondered where someone would get what appeared to be an authentic sword from the Middle Ages. I didn't ask any questions, though the oddity of a real samurai sword falling off a truck in front of me on the road some years previous did enter my mind, but you'd be amazed how blank your mind goes to asking questions when people show up at your ranch to confront a band of rogue gray aliens. Almost everything seems normal the moment you accept that original premise.

I escorted Brandy and the two men she had brought with her into my ranch. Brandy immediately tuned into a very negative energy. She began to cleanse the house. Upon entering the room where the suicide had taken place, she immediately sensed the young man. She told me the young man had shot himself and his spirit had been in the house since that time. I confirmed to her that indeed a seventeen-year-old boy had put a shotgun in his mouth on his graduation day from high school. Brandy and the two Jays prayed over him and sent him as much love as they could. The wall I was standing beside began to heat up. It got so hot I thought it was going to burst into flames. Brandy told the boy it's time to move on as she and her Sirian companions prayed intensely, and she heard a voice say, *that's the most love I have ever felt.* Then he left. I told Brandy that I had intermittently felt the human spirit in the house from time to time, but it was so difficult to distinguish from the other stuff going on. I remember when I was doing renovations on the house, I tore up the floor in the room the boy had killed himself, and there was still blood on the concrete.

I should take a moment here to explain what Brandy told me. Very often when a human being dies in a tragedy they have difficulty moving on because of the weight they carry on the other side. Here we are talking about the astral body. Some people might refer to it as the light body or the translucent body. It's the form we all have right after the physical body. It's associated with our feelings and sensory data. Just as the physical body can get overloaded with food and unable to move well, the astral body can get saturated with negative emotions and stuck in a position after death, and again, this is most common in violent and sudden deaths where there is very strong emotion.

The person has tremendous difficulty changing their vibration because to do so they have to completely digest what they did, accept it, forgive themselves, and begin to allow love back into them. That Mexican boy had been in my house for fifteen years. When I saw Brandy do what she did — release the boy — I felt a little impotent as a spiritual being. This poor kid had been serving a penance in my house for a decade and a half and there was nothing I could do for him. Joyce and I had felt him on occasion, but the subtle differences between fourth dimensional presences was not something we had learned to discern early on. For a long time at the ranch it was all just under the umbrella of *weird*. It stunned me when Brandy came into my home and immediately dealt with the boy. She knew the generalities without any assistance from me — a young boy had died violently in the room. I told her about the family that farmed cattle, the high school graduation, and the shotgun.

Even now, as I tell this story within my story, I remember that I forgot to ask why he killed himself. I guess it doesn't matter. I suspect that the aliens influenced him. They can induce depression, anger, and suicide ultimately. In the end, the battle was territorial. The aliens didn't want any humans living at the ranch. I had to learn that my moods were being influenced, that the anger and rage I would feel, the absolute bewilderment and frustration when they would disappear car keys and cell phones, was them trying to push me off the ranch any way they could, which is probably what the young man succumbed to at the ranch. It never ceases to amaze me how human consciousness in the subtle forms, like the astral body, can affect physical reality.

It makes you pause and think of all the deaths, divorces, and incarcerations that might have been influenced by the other side, and it makes me think of we human beings, our petty egos, our pride, and our insensitivity. These extraordinary teachers come to the planet — Abraham, Jesus, Muhammad, Milarepa, and Kabir, to name a few — and our human tendencies and vulgarities create robed professionals who argue doctrine like insurance underwriters disputing a claim. It's sickening how ill the human race is, how spiritually ill we are, and how many people have been forced onto pharmaceuticals and told they are mentally ill when in fact they are not hearing voices or seeing things; they are being attacked from the fourth dimension.

The ranch became a spiritual crucible for me, a realignment of my life priorities, and a consecration to the divine. When the young man left my home, he did so because he allowed love and forgiveness into him. While he was there, I could feel him from time to time. It wasn't a malicious presence. He didn't want to hurt Joyce or I. He just wanted to be left alone. It's another reminder that it is very important that we love ourselves and work through all of our emotional conditions in life. How many people are locked in a stasis in the afterlife? How we die is extremely important.

One the most famous near-death experiences in the twentieth century was that of a fellow by the name of Dannion Brinkley. He was struck by lightning a number of times in his life. I think he died three times. He wrote several books and described exactly what Brandy was telling me in my home after she cleared the young Mexican boy out. How important it is for us to live our lives truly and correctly and to stay in a good emotional place and, most importantly, to allow love into us.

As we get into the subtler bodies that exist inside of us and we occupy after death, it's important that we understand that love determines where we go and where we fit in after the body fails. Love is a kind of fuel on the other side that allows us to move. It gives us a lightness so that we can rise up to better worlds. The heaviness of a life laden with guilt and negative emotions fixes us to certain positions very close to the physical world, often very close to the area that the last act of hate or aggression took place. It could be one explanation for purgatory, and it certainly explains ghosts, or at least part of it. One of the very many beautiful things that Brinkley did with his life was set up a hospice system in the United States, a place where people could go and die if they did not have family, a place where they could be loved before they passed the world, a place where they could let love into them. Very beautiful indeed.

The Portals

After that rather dramatic incident, which was just the beginning of Brandy's visit — we hadn't even begun to deal with the portals or the extraterrestrials yet — I took her to the room where I believed the portal was. She did some work in clearing the area. When I say work, I mean she would close her eyes and a very intense look would come over her face, and she would sort of quietly whisper in prayer. After some long minutes of this, she asked us all to sit around the coffee table, so we all went over to the coffee table, me, Brandy, and the two men that she called the two Jays. She told me that she had been instructed to *hold a space*. This was to allow the opening of a portal that she herself created. She explained that it provided a hologram for benevolent beings to come through, and Brandy told me that they wanted to speak to me. They had specific messages for me.

What I saw happen next was quite astounding. A sort of globe appeared above the table. It was like a hologram from a movie, or a computer generated interface, otherworldly. Then three beings came through. They were wearing breastplates and armor, and they had swords. I know what this sounds like, however, I have an obligation to report the truth, and I am telling you the truth. I long ago gave up any feeling about being embarrassed by speaking in public about what I have experienced. People need to know there's more to this world and our existence than what our senses and mind show us, much more. I can only tell you what I saw and what happened, no more, no less. I have no idea why higher order beings from another dimension, another world, would be brandishing weapons and armor more typical of seven hundred years ago in our human history, but they were. Brandy herself does not remember the incident too well. When she opens a portal like that and becomes *the space holder*, she's in another place and not really present to observe what's going on through the space that she's keeping open. I had to tell her what happened later on.

The Ships

We went outside when Brandy stopped *holding the space*. She went and spoke to the horses. She has the ability to communicate with animals. They told her their version of what had been happening on the ranch, the mutilations, the negative beings. Brandy explained to me that they could kill my animals but I was off limits, as was Joyce. She explained a cosmology in which there were not so much rules but consequences.

If they killed human beings they invoked a countermeasure from beings capable of dealing with them more effectively than a human being, so, in fear of that confrontation, they only tried to influence us, frighten us, torment us, keep us so psychologically imbalanced that we decided to leave the ranch, which was theirs as they saw it, not the actual house or the stables or the kennels, but the portals on the property, which they perceived as theirs because they knew how to use them. It's not like Joyce and I were putting on our dancing shoes and time traveling through interdimensional doors on weekends. In a weird way I understood the position of the grays. Taking the land from us was like taking a diamond from a monkey in the jungle — what use did the monkey have for the diamond — it's just that in this case the diamond was our home, even though we didn't see any value in it other than a home.

Brandy walked the property line, all the while doing what she called *energy work*, which was raising the vibration to make it more difficult for non love-centered entities to come onto my property. Then we went to the front of the property, close to where the metal gate is located. It was there that Brandy felt a very strong presence of the grays. Those were the ones, as she put it, that she decided to *negotiate* with. She did some blessings, and then she and her two Jays turned around to face the south. I turned to look as well. The sky was a beautiful shade of orange, almost like a tangerine color, and then I saw a plethora of ships uncloak. It was astounding. I could not believe the size of them. One of them must have been the size of two or three city blocks. We turned and faced the east and that's when the mothership came into view. I'm not even going to try and describe how big it was. It was like a city floating in the sky. Brandy began to speak.

It wasn't English. I don't know what language she was speaking. It sounded like Klingon from the Star Trek television show, low and guttural, like Mongolian throat singing without the melody. She told me later that she was still in a trance state. She spoke directly to the grays, ordered them to leave the property, notified them that if they surrendered they'd be treated well. They would be escorted to what Brandy defined as the equivalent of a *reform school*. The whole thing played out like an interdimensional High Noon with her as the sheriff, but she wasn't outgunned. The ships that had uncloaked were to let the grays know what they were facing — a show of force. The grays at Stardust Ranch were defined time and time again as a *rogue* group. This is an important point and it needs some explanation. Very often in the world of exopolitics we perceive alien races as completely uniform and homogeneous.

While it is true they do have more of a hive mind than humans, extraterrestrial races are as diverse as the human race. We have everything from leaders of criminal organizations to holy people in the human race. The same dichotomy exists in the other races. I was told that the rogue group of grays on my property was living there because they were attracted by the high vibration of the portal. There were three ships with about twenty grays on each ship for a total of sixty rogue grays, apparently very attached to the portals on my property, and especially the one portal that had the time dimension, either past or future. I had already killed a number of them, maybe close to a dozen, by the time that Brandy came out with her to warriors from Sirius.

Lightning Strikes

The low guttural language that Brandy was speaking went on for quite some time, at least ten minutes. I had no idea what was being said or who was listening to it. I could tell by her disposition and the disposition of the two Sirian warriors that she had brought, the two Jays, that things were not going as well as they wanted them to go as far as a peaceful negotiation. I noticed that clouds had begun to form directly above us, dark, charcoal colored clouds that seemed full of water. It was too sudden for it to be a natural phenomenon. Something was bringing the clouds together right above us at the ranch. Amidst this unknown language of the three parties on the ground, Brandy and the two Jays, they formed a circle at one point and all of them raised their swords. They weren't just decorations. They weren't role playing Dungeons and Dragons. I later learned that swords are an archetypal weapon in the cosmos, representing truth and honor and the willingness to fight from the heart, as opposed to camping out a thousand yards away and shooting someone with a sniper rifle, I suppose. Swords meant you fought for the truth and you fought with honor. It makes me rethink the entire notion that the archangels are allegorical beings as opposed to literal.

At this point in the negotiations all three of them raised their swords and touched the tips, and, at that exact moment, a bolt of purple lightning came down and struck the ground several feet away from the trio. It was a loud, booming sound, disorienting and utterly baffling. My mind went blank for about ten seconds, the way I imagine a person blanks close to an explosion. I felt like I was beside myself, looking on the whole surreal affair as a serene and detached observer, then I snapped back into my body, and my mind reminded me of what had just happened. They were all as directly affected as me.

Brandy was profoundly disoriented. There was a circular black scorch mark on the ground, maybe three feet in diameter. The two Sirian warriors left with Brandy almost immediately, with Brandy looking at me and saying, I don't think they'll bother you anymore, as she strode away. She seemed a little *off* to me. It was not until a few days later that I was able to speak to Brandy on the telephone. She had no knowledge of being struck by lightning, but something had happened. The energy from the purple bolt had traveled through the ground and through the cork soles of her footwear, and it had affected her somehow. She was having memory problems. She told me that she had been visited by the Men in Black[1].

She was told in no uncertain terms that she was not to speak publicly about what happened at Stardust Ranch on July 31th, 2011. With God as my witness and all that I hold sacred in life, as crazy as these details sound, as outlandish as they sound, as storybook as they sound, they happened just as I am telling you they happened. In later weeks I heard from Brandy that one of the Sirians had gone crazy. He started to hear voices and see things and had to be institutionalized. The other Sirian took his family and went underground, completely off the grid.

We stirred something up at the ranch. I later heard through a network of common acquaintances that it took three or four years for Brandy to get normal after the lightning strike. Vast portions of her memory were taken from her. The presence of the rogue grays abated a little, but it never went away. The abductions stopped for the most part. It seemed as though some kind of a truce had been struck. But the idea of the grays being removed and turned over to a reform institution in the galactic council did not happen. To this day I really don't know what happened on that fateful day, July 31th, 2011. The only thing I know for sure is that my life changed dramatically. Once I met benign extraterrestrials through Brandy, they became a part of my life. I will get into that in a subsequent chapter.

---

[1]MacDonald Note. I asked Brandy Howe when I interviewed her what the Men in Black are. She told me she could not tell me, that this information was not timed to come out yet.

The Sirians

The beings from Sirius are known throughout the Milky Way Galaxy and beyond as warriors and protectors. They are relied upon to effect forced change on beings who are creating profound disturbances like the grays at my ranch. It's important to note here how Brandy defined the two warriors from Sirius. They were human beings. They were born on this world. They grew up on this world. When Brandy says they were two warriors from Sirius, she is saying that they were walk-ins. A walk-in occurs when a human life commences and the soul that occupies the body has made a contract to vacate the body at a certain point and switch places with another being who then walks in and takes over the body and lives the life. This was a very important point for me to get my head around.

The questions that brought me to resolution were the result of Brandy telling me the consequences for the two warriors from Sirius that came to my ranch. One of them went briefly insane. The other one had a family and had to go into hiding for a while. The threats from the powers-that-be in the dark side of the exopolitics world, the side of the exopolitics world that nobody speaks about, were so great that he was in fear for his life and the life of his family.

So let's get a proper definition of what a walk-in is. It would not be unfair to say that walk-in is a new age term. I don't like to use the phrase new age. It bothers me tremendously for some reason. It seems to me that it has become as ridiculous and contradictory as the traditional religions. However, I don't see any way of avoiding this. The term definitely comes into vogue through the new age community in the latter part of the twentieth century.

In typical form, the military-industrial-entertainment complex — read Hollywood here — addresses the idea of a walk-in, and specifically an extraterrestrial walk-in, in the film adaptation of the novel *K-Pax*. The novel was written by a gentleman named Gene Brewer and published in 1995. The film followed in 2001 and starred Kevin Spacey. In the film Spacey is a man under the supervision of a psychiatrist played by Jeff Bridges. It's actually a remake of an earlier film called *The Man facing Southeast*, made in 1986 in Argentina. It is entirely possible that Gene Brewer ripped off the premise for the novel from the original Argentine film. But I certainly don't want to digress here into a diatribe on plagiarism. Let's stick with the Kevin Spacey film, K-Pax.

Spacey's character is named Prot. He presents a beguiling conundrum for his psychiatrist, Jeff Bridges. The film allows the viewer to explore the idea of a walk-in. Prot is an extraterrestrial walk-in who stepped into a body at a moment of suicide. He revived the body and continued existence with the being inside completely changed. If all of this sounds a little bit fantastical, even the Tibetan Buddhists talk about walk-ins. It has been a part of their culture for centuries.

The easiest way to come to a comprehension of what a walk-in is is to watch the film K-Pax. For the purposes of this narrative, I have done all I can to present the definition, and we must accept that the two warriors from Sirius were walk-ins, part of a contract made with the human souls before they incarnated. I am in no position to disagree with Brandy, nor am I inclined to contest the narrative. It not only seems plausible to me, but likely.

Brandy the White

It was just when I started working on this book in 2019 that I got more detail on Brandy. She and I had lost touch. We tried to stay in touch for the first year after she came out here, I live very close in Phoenix, but something always seemed to get in our way, as though we were not supposed to be communicating. I heard through my co-writer, Bruce McDonald, who did all the interviews for the novel, that Brandy regarded the event at my Ranch as an initiation.

In spiritual and occult paths an initiation is the sudden endowment of a new realization. Initiations are usually disorienting and difficult. Consciousness does not come easy for the human race. Most of the people I know who have developed any kind of clairvoyant ability have done so through intense trial, very often a long and protracted struggle with a mortal disease, or a long, intense psychological turmoil, like being abducted on a regular basis by gray aliens. It's a combination of the stress of remembering the abductions when the memories do come back and the consistent transportation to the fourth dimension where the abductions take place.

All human beings are interdimensional. And many of the dreams people have at night are on another dimension, usually the astral plane. But abduction takes more of the waking mind into the fourth dimension. People who meditate regularly for years often develop perceptual abilities well beyond the norm.

The engagement by Brandy with the gray aliens was another kind of initiation. The purple lightning struck the ground close enough to her that she was deeply affected by the energy. I later found out that it traveled underground and went right into her body. She developed new ways of perceiving reality and new understandings. Whatever happened at my ranch on July 31st, 2011, like Gandalf in the movie *Lord of the Rings: The Fellowship of the Ring*, Brandy came out at a certain level of consciousness and left at a new level of consciousness that would take her some time, several years, to rebalance into herself. If you remember the movie, the Challenge that Gandalf the Gray faced was the Balrog, the ancient fiery demon in the underground, both Gandalf and the Balrog fall into a Chasm and engage in mortal combat. Gandalf prevails and returns from the chasm as Gandalf the White. He has new powers and a new mission. Brandy documents her own experience on my Ranch on her website.

Dr. Brandy's Personal Lightning Testimonial

On July 31st, 2011, I was indirectly struck by lightning. The lightning entered through the ground behind me and surfaced up through my heels and went out through the top of my head.

Five days after the strike I was given a message from the Above which said.

You need to do Lightning Therapy.

I asked What is Lightning Therapy?

As I always get answers; I was baffled as none came. I ended my meditation with the statement. I guess that you will just tell me, when I need to know.

The very next day, I walked into a metaphysical store that I worked at three days per week and there were twenty Fulgurites sitting on the back table. I was in awe, so to speak, as I looked at these specimens which said on their box: Lightning In A Box!

That is when I started my research on Fulgurites and was awakened to the mystical, magical and practical powers if you will, that these awesome tubes hold.

If anyone of you has the Crystal Bible Two, Fulgurite is listed in there with it's awesome properties. The Crystal Bibles (Judy Hall) are available on Amazon.com and many metaphysical stores as well.

166

Approximately, two weeks after the lightning strike, I started experiencing many physical issues. I developed a hematoma and subsequently started bleeding through my nose, mouth and then vaginally. (As I had a hysterectomy some 30 years ago, that event stirred up my curiosity, if you will, as to why this was all happening.) In my research, I found that it was not uncommon for bleeding to occur due to the lightning damaging blood vessels, which could later break, from the impact of the strike.

I then started to experience memory loss, dizziness, loss of vision, confusion and what can best be described as haziness as I moved through my daily routines.

As it came to a head one day, my employer refused to let me return to work until I went to the hospital emergency. I reluctantly obliged as I was feeling that I was ready to check out if you will. I did not have insurance and I knew that this was going to be a very expensive trip.

My trip to the hospital was also very unpleasant as I described to the doctors why I was there; they looked at me like I was crazy and accused me of being on drugs. For the record, I have never taken drugs in this lifetime!

They were very rude and condescending, to say the least.

I was happy that I had brought my camera and provided them with some proof of the occurrence. They still did not get it as they kept saying:

If you got hit by lightning, you would be dead! Well, not everyone that gets hit by lightning dies, if you will, but everyone, I can guarantee you, has a life changing experience!

It was shortly thereafter that The Thirteen Universal Beings of Light started downloading me with information on using the Fulgurites with other healing crystals and guided me on how to use them for my healing and subsequently, guided me to help others to do the same.

Through Divine Guidance, I have now encompassed the Fulgurites, along with several other Extremely powerful and scarce Crystals to promote Healing, Relieving Blockages, Brain Rewiring and Chakra Activation.[2]

___

[2]https://www.nitestarlifeawareness.com/-Lightning-Therapy-.html

Part V

My New World

Chapter 18

Contact

Some say that in this life to experience anything really good you have to experience something bad. The laws of duality dictate that you don't even know that something is sweet unless you have tasted bitter. You can't really understand what beauty is until you know what ugliness is. The same holds true for my experiences with extraterrestrials.

I couldn't really understand what a benign extraterrestrial was until I experienced malignant extraterrestrials. After a decade and a half of a living hell with the gray aliens and the assorted weirdness at the ranch my life changed. The visit by doctor Brandy opened a whole new book in my life. I had no experience with positive extraterrestrials.

I didn't know that somebody could come to your house with two Sirians. It was a life-changing event. I became and I remain a contactee. A contactee, as already described in this book, is someone contacted by benign extraterrestrials. Benign simply means non-invasive, cooperative, and compliant with a set of laws they claim the universe operates upon.

There are a number of famous contactees in the exopolitics world. They're not household names, far from it, but they are very well-known in the exopolitics world, and, according to them, they are very well known by the governments that want to suppress the spread of extraterrestrial knowledge, and they are known by the negative extraterrestrials.

When Brandy and I sat in the living room, she opened up a ball of light, a portal she created. From this portal emerged two more beings. One was an Andromedan. The other was a reptilian. I engaged in a dialogue with them that lasted some hours. This is not to say that some hours passed at the ranch. Interacting with these beings changes the flow of time.

A two or three minute interaction with these beings can come to represent three or four hours of time in your mind as you unpack the information. It's a little like a zip file on a computer. Once you open it up it's got much more data than it's size suggests. The following is my account of what I was told by the positive extraterrestrials. I should point out as well that my contact has not stopped. It's ongoing.

Portals

I asked what the portals were. They told me they were doorways through time and space. Doorways through space are quite common. They are all over the planet. Time travel portals that can go to the future or the past are very rare. They wouldn't tell me how many there were on the planet. It was like this with every topic.

They answered my questions, but in a way that opened up a dozen new questions, with none of the subsequent questions addressed. There was none of the intuitive flow a conversation has with a human being. Everything was stilted, and it had to be pried out.

The portal on the back of my property was put where it is eight thousand years ago. It is directly connected with Egypt, which, according to what the extraterrestrials told me, was a far more expansive culture than people have been led to believe. The portal has automatic activation times, and it can be activated at any time by someone who knows how to operate it.

The portals are an electrical anomaly, or, rather, anomalous to human beings in the reality we live, but normal to other beings. It was made clear to me that when a race lives in more than one dimension their sense of time is not linear. Time moves and expresses itself differently in the fourth dimension, the dimension where extraterrestrials live and pass through, and a dimension many humans travel through, either consciously by practice, as was the case with Robert Monroe, author of *Journeys out of the Body*, or unconsciously when they sleep and dream.

In a sense, it was made clear to me that a human being is a series of portals through energy centers in our bodies, the chakra system, but the portal on my property physically transported people. When we travel consciously or in our sleep we are traveling in our subtle body. It's a form similar to our physical body but lighter, and, from the perspective of the earth, it's translucent, but, while we are in the fourth dimension, it's not. It has something approximating physicality as we experience it here on the earth, with slight differences to accommodate that dimension.

This explained much of what had been seen on the ranch. I had been sitting in the living room in the past, had the portal open up, and seen ancient Egypt inside, as well as Rome and other civilizations. I'd also had human beings come through the portal and march about the ranch for a while. I've had native shamans and Roman Centurions. There's really no end to what fourth dimensional being might show up. I was told not to use it. In many ways the extraterrestrials viewed me as a dog, or a horse.

I get the sense interacting with them that they don't have a high regard for our race. I feel tolerated a lot of the time. Again, I'm not saying they're cold. They have a good presence. It is uplifting to be around them. I just felt like a child dealing with adults. The contextual gaps in our realities are so great they need to be factored into everything they say.

Human Growth

One of the first things that I asked the extraterrestrials about was human growth. I wanted to know if the growth cycle we were going through is natural. Here I am referring to the last hundred years or so, beginning at World War I and leading up to our present day where we seem intent on destroying ourselves and the world. I suggested that we were about eight hundred years behind in our development due to the confines of religion during the Middle Ages.

They told me that in fact it was much worse, that we were thousands of years behind our development cycle. What was particularly engaging about their dissertation was the way in which it forced me to contextualize what growth was. The creation of a sentient life-form on a planet at the density we live at, which we can call three dimensional for the purposes of our context, is the crowning achievement of the life process on a planet. Here we need to define sentience.

It is the ability to have enough awareness to say that you exist. We can look upon this as the philosophical self-awareness of the French philosopher, Descarte — *I think therefore I am*. This has nothing to do with self-awareness as it is defined spiritually. That's a whole other topic, but, for the purposes of this explanation, self-awareness is the conscious understanding that you are an individuated being, you think therefore you are. According to the extraterrestrials, the first level of growth in awareness on a planet is mastery of the planet because the sentient life-form, in the case of earth, the human being, is the steward of the planet.

As the steward the human being is supposed to be able to communicate with everything in visible creation. I know, I was slack-jawed when I heard it, too. We are supposed to be able to communicate with animals, reptiles, insects, trees, and everything that is living on the planet. This is regarded as an elementary step in the evolution of a sentient being.

These things must be understood before a sentient being is allowed into the solar system and then allowed into the galaxy. How many people do you know who can communicate with animals? I know one, the woman who came out to my ranch to negotiate with the rogue gray aliens. The biosphere that we live in is all a product of the same creator that made us. As stewards of the planet we are supposed to be listening to the other life-forms and aiding them in their existence.

As I was listening to them I was reminded of a Hopi prophecy that stated the world would not have balance until the native peoples and the Europeans came to an understanding and appreciation of each other. This was supposed to happen when we came to America. Something went terribly wrong. Rather than listen to and learn from the natives, and vice-versa, they listening to us and learning from us, to create a more whole people, we engaged in brutal warfare that has left the native population almost decimated.

The natives on the planet represent the best possible example of stewardship and communion with nature. It's only recently that the white man and other races have begun communing more properly with the natives, unfortunately this has to be done at a chemical level with psychedelics administered by the natives, such as ayahuasca, which has become quite popular in certain circles in the West and often referred to as the god vine.

Natives for their part should have adopted more advanced forms of agriculture practiced by the Europeans, recognizing that it was egotistical of a tribal people to believe they could roam vast swatches of land and hunt a healthy population of wild, undomesticated game. Their model of existence did not allow for population growth. It's a two-way street. It's not all the evil white man or the savage Indian. It's a failure to communicate and understand each other. It's a failure to build a bridge and to make two cultures better and more balanced.

If any of this sounds far-fetched, let me assure you that I watched Brandy walk around my ranch and talk to all of the individual animals and tell me what they were thinking and what ailed them. Given that she didn't know their medical histories, I can only conclude that she effectively communicated with them. It's difficult for me at this point after witnessing it myself to believe that human beings are not able to communicate with animals. Canada has produced a relatively famous ethnobotanist named Wade Davis, who was National Geographic's explorer-in-residence for a number of years. Some of you may have seen the film, *Serpent and the Rainbow*, about Voodoo and creating zombies in Haiti. That was based on the work of Wade Davis.

Davis spent a number of years living with tribal people in the Amazon Rainforest. He was curious to know how aboriginal cultures had come to an understanding of plants that allowed them to prepare medicines and hallucinogenics for ritual that were so complicated they would be difficult to replicate in a sterile laboratory at an Ivy League university. The natives told Davis that the plants talk to them.

The fact that the human race has conditioned itself to acquire property and wealth is precisely what is blocking us from our growth potential. I don't think they mean we should all become like Francis of Assisi and give away all of our possessions. I think what they meant was that these things should not govern us. We should live to eat nutritiously and have safe and comfortable shelter in our lives, but we should be able to let go of those things and travel and do other things in life when we need or want to.

They stressed that we need to be unencumbered on this planet, and by unencumbered they meant not held back by anything, and they stressed this quite a bit, telling me that when we were unencumbered we would be able to live most of the time at our most heightened state of awareness. This in turn would create a purposeful perception that would permit us to grow. Our entire lives have come to be consumed by what we own.

The extraterrestrials explained to me that human beings seem to want to collect things, in a sense, they were telling me that human beings were hoarders. It's the absolute worst possible thing you can do. It prevents us from being able to move around freely, meet all kinds of new people, see new environments, and experience new things. They stressed the idea that our world is our wealth. The entire construction is a classroom.

The planet is our wealth. It's a living construction. We are part of the same life construction. We are at the top of the creational process on this planet. The way it was explained to me by the extraterrestrials, everything in creation has the purpose of teaching. All of the teaching is to bring us closer to the creator. At times, as I listened to these fellows, it almost sounded shamanic. The Hopi people say that they came to this planet through a tunnel. I have these tunnels on my ranch.

Institutions

Anything that is institutionally taught to us to put us on a treadmill for decades is inherently negative. It runs counter to the way a human being is supposed to live in accordance with our own nature. We're not supposed to do anything except be the very best we can be and try to be happy. Our happiness should not be about acquisition, it should be about process. We don't trust own value enough. We are capable of having profound spiritual growth, and profound spiritual experience, and we can share it with each other.

The problem is we don't trust what we experience. If it doesn't have the rubber stamp of approval from a church or a university or an institution, we don't trust what we get from the inside. All of our experiences are valuable. The good and the bad. We need to learn to take those experiences and understand them for what they really are, not to live in them forever. Absorb the experience and move on. The thing that we have the tendency to do most is not move on. We dwell on things too long. It takes us too long to process information. All of the information that we process is coming from the external.

The force that is working against us for the most part is doubt. We don't invest in ourselves. We believe that somebody else is supposed to tell us who we are. Most people would rather believe in an authority figure or someone here who has already achieved a certain level of success. We don't believe in ourselves. When you do that the best you can become is a copy of somebody else. Given what we are, as the extraterrestrials explained it to me, it's the equivalent of spiritual cloning or life cloning. It's not an authentic way to live. Our life selections are a form of our consumer tendencies. Our children are expected to choose their lives by a certain age.

Hothouse

It gets worse. Forces are working against us. I'm not talking about the Biblical devil, but perhaps something close. What I'm talking about here is the truth of the human race. We're a genetically manipulated species. Planet earth is a hothouse where extraterrestrial races grow what they need here and transplant it to other planets. There's not a lot of concern for anything other than usefulness. There are literally hundreds of thousands of other worlds to which human beings are transplanted. We're placed on a planet and put in a certain set of circumstances and given a master program and then the same sequences repeat themselves. This is why the Hopi creation story has them walking through a portal and coming to planet earth.

This has been done to us by races which are more aware. The first step in advancement is not technological. It's a breakthrough in awareness. It's the realization that we are multi-dimensional beings. The next great advancement for the human race should be an esoteric advancement, a spiritual advancement, not an exoteric advancement, not another manifestation in our three-dimensional reality — another bloody smart phone, a television with better resolution, a faster computer, or artificial intelligence. If we don't balance ourselves we will crash and burn again, as so many human civilizations have already, the last being Atlantis. I can't stress this dimensional breakthrough enough.

It's absolutely critical that this be understood. Without this understanding nothing is going to change. The seeders create a biological product, and they do it in accordance with whatever the climate and environment is of the planet on which they seed a *human*. Next, they create a context, and then they create a narrative. Once this seeding is done, the seeders walk away for ten thousand years and let the cycle take its course. There are very rarely any deviations from what they set up.

The more advanced races in our galaxy have life spans that far exceed a human lifespan. There are extraterrestrial races who live thousands of years, some of them tens of thousands. Beyond that, reincarnation is real, a universal spiritual principle, and a healthy race has recall of their primary identity, the being that is reincarnating, what we might call the soul.

There is no extraterrestrial creator of the soul. This is fundamental. It must be understood if we are to escape the hell that has been human life on this planet. When you look at the wisdom that has visited this planet in the form of the great beings who seemed to embody a knowledge far beyond their life spans; it's because human beings have a consciousness that relates to subtler bodies that have this longer memory. Our very construction is transdimensional, but we are taught that to entertain this idea is insane. What is insane is dismissing our transdimensionality.

For those of you who are angry or confused by what I am saying about human beings and their creation, I fall back on the metaphor of electricity. Nobody can define what electricity is. It's fundamental character is beyond understanding. We can harness it, move it, store it, ration it, and deploy it, but it's a mystery. Electrical engineers create transformers, circuits, fuses, blockers, and grounding systems, all in an attempt to use electricity. This is a one to one analogy to the spiritual nature of man. We are the electricity created by the universe.

The bodies and genetics the extraterrestrials create are the equivalent of what the electrical engineers do. In this metaphor the electricity is the spirit. The spirit cannot be controlled or altered. It just is. the same is true for the soul. It just is. It comes from the creator and the creator is outside all time and space. It just is. We are equal to all other sentient beings in creation. The only difference is our evolution in this three-dimensional reality. In that regard, many of the beings aware of us are eons more advanced than us in terms of understanding the appendages of the soul, the body, the feelings, the memory, and the mind. If you listen closely to what the benign extraterrestrials told me, it's a one to one match for the spiritual teachers who have incarnated on the planet. The cosmic brotherhood of sentient beings is aligned with the best of our spiritual teachings.

Time and time again we view the extraterrestrial phenomenon as external: an alien, a ship, transferred technology, the rogue grays at my ranch, the portals, and secret government files. Most extraterrestrial contact is internal. It's a thought we don't know the origin of or a vivid dream.

How the World Changes

I spoke to the extraterrestrials about the state of the world and the environment. I wanted to know if there is any way to turn things around. I certainly don't believe the climate change narrative being pushed by the globalist agenda. It's a fraud. However, we do have many problems on this planet related to overconsumption and overextraction of resources,like the endless wars for energy resources like oil. What could possibly be done? Time and time again I was told the same thing. We have everything we need to live harmoniously and sustainably on this planet. The only thing blocking us is our lack of belief in ourselves. I found this astounding. They told me we had been conditioned to external authority, but internal direction was the way to harmonize with ourselves and our environment.

It was a little frustrating dealing with them. Everything seemed to be this riddle, like a Haiku poem. They stressed fractals, small communities, experimental living, cooperative self-government on a microscale, but with self-discipline. I thought about the hippie movement. They were sabotaged by hedonism, an aborted dream by lack of follow through. Indian ashrams get it right in some measure. The Scottish ecovillage, Findhorn, is an excellent example. Look it up. It's a community that is self-sustaining and focused on human development. People who go on retreats there report many transdimensional experiences.

What about help? Why weren't the extraterrestrials helping us? The answer is simple: certain conditions must be in the human race for help to be offered. We have to take responsibility for ourselves, then the help will be understood. The help is always here. It's inside us. We just don't listen or pay attention to our inner lives. There are too many people in the exopolitics world asking the extraterrestrials to land, declare themselves in our visible spectrum, and solve all our problems with advanced technology, but what would prevent the problems from recurring in a number of human generations? If the thought and feeling patterns that created the problems aren't dealt with first then no solution would be lasting, and we would be making our extraterrestrial saviors our parole officers, and they don't want a custodial relationship with a sentient race. Their thinking is completely different. There's no quid pro quo, nothing in it for them.

It is true that in the subtle worlds our lives are interconnected, and, therefore, our actions on this planet affect them, especially when we get into things like fission and fusion. The extraterrestrial presence spikes after the nuclear bombs in the Second World War. It also sent a signal out to the galaxy and the universe that we're here. The human race does not tread softly, and not all extraterrestrial races are benign. There are things out there more frightening than the demons of our religions, and far more disturbing and destructive than the rogue grays that terrorized Joyce and I. The difference is between being saved and being sovereign. Extraterrestrials are more than willing to help us become sovereign, but sovereignty means owning your cause and effect cycles, learning by experience. So when we as a race of beings, the human race on planet earth, say we want help, to the extraterrestrials the first response is why are you not using the help built into you? From their perspective, we're dying of thirst beside a pristine mountain stream. It's ludicrous, but infancy is what it is, and we are still an infant race.

The best way forward is intentional living from the ground up. Micro-communities that don't sabotage themselves are an excellent starting point. Sabotage here means what the baby boomers did in the sixties. It has to be a disciplined approach. This creates the environment for growth. The next question is what is growth? It's the movement into consciousness and the transdimensionality of our species. It's coming to understand what spirit is in a literal way, not the endless allegories that are the favorite of religions.

Spirit is not an allegory, just as electricity is not an allegory. Spirit is the breath of the creator exhaled into time and space, and experienced by us as sound and light. We take it like play dough and mold it into fantasies that fulfill our basest desires. Sit quietly with your eyes closed for thirty minutes a day. You'll see your spirit. It's all the thoughts and feelings you've populated your consciousness with, the things that are giving you hypertension and ulcers and cancer. Behind the creations in your consciousness is the indiscriminate, unconditional spirit from the creator, the first sound, if you will, and remember sound is movement. We live in a sound and light universe. Light is really a form of sound. The primary quality of the creator is sound.

What would happen in the internal world of a human being in which desire was muted? What pictures would take the place of the aforementioned fantasies of most human beings? Object pictures is the answer. You would have elementary clairvoyance. Extraterrestrial contact is not just disks and dead aliens and my ranch. It's also dreams and visions. To understand it all you need to understand what the mystics have been trying to tell us as well, people like Jacob Bohme, Rumi, and Zoroaster, to name a few. In classical Western philosophy we define the subjective and objective as the internal and external. The things that happen inside our heads and the things that happen in the world. This is erroneous. The real definition of subjective and objective is our creations and the creations of others, including extraterrestrials and the spiritual governors — the gods — and the creator itself.

Nothing human beings invent is original. Creation is finished. It was finished the moment it began, because it started outside of time and space, therefore, anything we create is only a manifestation in our three dimensional reality of something already created, if only in the universal mind as a concept laying dormant in the consciousness of a developing species like human beings. So what do we strive for? What exactly makes life worth living? Our goal is to become the best we can be. Learn as much as we can. Grow as much as we can. The final stage is internal. Our external form is fixed, unless the fundamental components of our reality change, like gravity, the force of the sun, or if we decide to live underground, to name a few.

The way forward for us are independent communities where human beings define their own growth, their own environment, their own limitations, away from the crippling influence of an overly institutionalized world — the literal and diametric opposite of the direction the self-serving power structures controlling the world are taking us. It's going to take courage, but courage is a foregone conclusion for survival on this planet going forward. It takes courage to stand against tear gas in a yellow vest protest in Paris. It takes courage to fight a superior invading army that wants your resources yet convinces the world they're liberating you from tyranny. It takes courage to live fully in a world where institutional propaganda conditions you to believe the world is ending.

There's no option left but courage, so why not make it active courage rather than reactive courage? Why not create your own life? Why not turn your back on the herd and graze alone? Is that not what the freedom of the West has always represented? The benefit of the *economies of scale* created in the twentieth century are lost if there is no equitable distribution of the wealth created. Complete state control to arrest the hoarding of the rich is not a solution. It inhibits the freedom of expression that makes a human life meaningful. That leaves self-defined living, people returning to land to sustain themselves. This mitigates the pollution of transportation. People don't realize that eighty percent of the world's oxygen comes from plankton in the oceans.

The American poultry industry sends chicken to China to be gutted and cleaned and then sent back to American supermarkets because the labor is so cheap it's a net profit for the corporate agriculture industry in the United States. Yet their propaganda convinces you to pay a carbon tax for using gasoline. Why have governments not come up with any taxing incentive or actuarial calculations that assess the environmental damage as part of the total cost of production, as in the China chicken cleaning example? Because our governments are not involved in solving any problems. They're involved in demonizing us for their failures.

Why is the burden for man-made climate change being taxed at the consumer level and unchallenged at the corporate level? The opportunity has never been greater for ecovillages because the incentive is so high. Continuing to live in the macro-models of western democracies is killing the planet, and no level of carbon taxing will turn it around. Extraterrestrial contact going forward is going to be with individual human beings and small groups. First contact was with governments, and they used everything given to them for their own benefit and power, not solutions for the people.

Spiritual Teachings

We have outgrown all our religions. There are some spiritual paths still useful on the planet, but we need to stop thinking in terms of liberation. The Dalai Lama claims a mission of rescuing all sentient beings from this planet? Why? If we think of our world as a prison then it is a prison. The extraterrestrials told me our spiritual goals are conjoined with our planet. The earth is our classroom. It is within us to create longevity. A longer physical life will produce more wisdom.

Transhumanism is not the way to go. Augmenting ourselves with tech hacks to our biology would be catastrophic. It would further mute our connection with the creator. They stressed over and over again that we have everything we need. I'm not quite sure I understand completely what they meant. They told me that we don't understand what imagination is, especially unpolluted imagination, which is imagination connected to awe and wonder, forcing questions. They told me that by creational law all questions must be answered, and therefore every question is its own answer. The question is more important than the answer.

At no point in the history of the human race since we began recording it in this cycle — about 8,000 years ago — have we been able to create a livable human environment, a place where people can live and not dream of a better place like heaven. This is not to be confused with thinking about death and what happens to a human being after death. That's completely natural. From the extraterrestrial perspective there is no such thing as death. There's only the translation from one form to another.

Reincarnation is the universally accepted spiritual paradigm. It's only in an incarnate form that we can fully realize everything in creation from the bottom to the top. All creatures in creation seek to have a body. The religions of this planet are escape plans. All of our philosophers, sages, prophets, and spiritual masters have told us the same thing time and time again: this planet is a living hell and we need to get out of here. I don't disagree that this planet is a living hell, but it's our hell, and only we can turn it into the kind of place that allows us to stop fantasizing about heaven.

Every aspect of human character has been designed and cultivated in this limited dimension in which we exist. The idea of cruelty, the idea of kindness, the idea of honor, all of them human constructs to survive in this dimension at its present frequency and its present reality. We assume that our values carry out into the universe, that they are in fact universal. This is not the case.

We ask ourselves, how could we be treated so badly? The first and most obvious answer is we treat ourselves this way. It doesn't matter what the influences are. The influences are part of the lesson. Everything that comes about is meant to come about. Tragedy does not exist in higher order civilizations. It's a human construct. Tragedy is spiritual pornography from the extraterrestrial perspective. It is the perversion of the normal. So much of our pain stems from our misunderstanding of life and death. If we understood death was only a transition we would understand how to live. Life and death are intertwined.

Life is the projection of events from another dimension. Some of our spiritual teachings explain this, but it is generally withheld from the human race on this planet. In the grand cosmology human life is about as revered as we revere a cockroach's. The disparity in consciousness and reality between the human race and some of these extraterrestrial races is so enormous it's like looking at two different orders of life. I'm not trying to speak negatively about the human race.

It's simply that we have to accept a reality. All life started out the way that we started out. The extension of life into the hundreds and then thousands of years is a quantum leap in terms of consciousness. Many of these extraterrestrial races look like us. They all follow the basic DaVinci form — man is the measure of all things. there is often a head, two arms, two legs, and a torso. Most of the beings have two eyes, a nose, a mouth, two ears, what the Taoists call the seven orifices above the neck, denoting an order of creation. Besides that there's absolutely nothing we have in common. Imagine a single human being alive for the last eight thousand years of history in one body. That human being would have been around to see everything that happened, If there had been one human being on the planet for the last eight thousand years we would have a complete and total understanding of what has happened on this planet. What would it be like to talk to a human being like that?

Conquering Fear

One of the things that the extraterrestrials stressed with me is the role fear plays in a given life. They describe fear as an absolutely useless emotion. Fear grounds consciousness. It exists in such great measure in human beings because we have not yet conquered death. Death is the baseline for all fear. It corrupts our imagination, and the imagination is a portal to other dimensions. Remember, all of creation is finished. It was finished the moment it began. Imagination is the place we view unmanifest reality, but that reality is corrupted by our fear. We are co-creators with creation. This is the meaning of human life. If fear is allowed to create in our imaginations then reality is corrupted, both the manifested and unmanifested realities.

They also told me that we neither understand nor use our imaginations correctly. The imagination is a communication tool between a human being and creation, and it is a whiteboard for our own creative processes. Ask any creative writer where their stories come from and they'll tell you they don't know. Or they'll defer to some amorphous entity like the *muse*. The same thing for scientific breakthroughs. Often the scientist can't really explain the breakthrough or how it happened. Creativity is the only thing artificial intelligence will lack. Our creativity is our connection with the creator, and the imagination is the language.

This becomes a critical understanding in extraterrestrial contact as well. Much of it happens in consciousness. Remember the academic reckoning between John Mack and his nemesis, Susan Clancy at Harvard? What was at the root of that dispute? The legitimacy of extraterrestrial contact and abductions. Mack postulated the experiences were real. When he says real he means *objective* experiences that need to be studied. What did Susan Clancy do? She put the experiences back in the box of the mind. In her analysis they were childhood trauma distilled into stories fueled by human desire, in her analysis the desire to believe you were special, that extraterrestrials had contacted you. She made them *subjective* experiences. What the extraterrestrials stressed with me was that there really is no subjective and objective when the imagination is properly understood. This explains things like talking to animals and plants, as Doctor Brandy Howe and Wade Davis, the ethnobotanist, explain.

Dreams are another aspect of our consciousness we don't understand yet. Active dreaming is visualizing. Passive dreaming happens when we sleep. Both are us communicating with our transdimensional selves. We have been taught to regard ourselves as ego structures. The ego, according to the extraterrestrials, is a psychic scab. Just as the skin will grow a scab when cut, so too does the psyche. We call it our ego. The problem is we don't let go of it when we're supposed to let go. We keep the psychic scab in place by never letting it heal, by constantly picking at it, by engaging our trauma long after trauma has ended. The bigger the trauma the bigger the ego. We've actually developed a culture around trauma in the West. This has tremendously weakened us. It's the equivalent of constantly breaking a bone when it's almost set and healed. We actually prefer to limp rather than walk at the level of consciousness. Why are so many of our soldiers committing suicide when they return from deployment? How does the Taliban treat PTSD? They don't. It doesn't exist in their culture. It's as if we invite the weakness into our lives by constantly picking at the scabs on our consciousness.

Symbiotic Living

There is a tremendous danger in this radical self-involvement in the West, especially now, this moment in our timeline. It prevents us from living symbiotically with the earth and the other life forms here. This is the biggest crisis in the world right now. It's not to be confused with man-made climate change, which is a hoax. It's about not separating ourselves from the world. Our consciousness is individuated. This is true, but this does not negate the fact that we are of this world while we are here. The world actually lends us the resources for an incarnation — air, earth, fire, water, and ether, which is the fifth element, and the one that has been held back from public knowledge.

Ether is the portal element, the one that allows us out of this three-dimensional reality into the other worlds. It goes by many names, prani to the Vedics, chi to the Taoists, ether in the Western mystery schools. That aside, the earth is the repository for the elements which compose our bodies, the vehicles we exist within when in this world. Our modern outlook has allowed us to forget this. The scab we have over our psyches, those egos we all pick at, they separate us from this basic understanding, and in this ignorance we are doing more and more damage to the ecosystem that allows us to exist.

Eco comes from the Greek oeco, which means household. We are destroying our home, and because our bodies are an aspect of this home, we are poisoning them as well. It's epidemic now. This awe inspiring interlinking of life we call the earth, completely symbiotic in its existence, is breaking down because we reject the symbiosis and imagine ourselves floating above it. It's the madness of ego. It cuts us off from symbiosis. Humility is required for symbiosis, and the ego is the antithesis of humility.

Everything in creation is self-regulating. The creation operates on fundamental principles. If they are violated warnings are given, but if the warning is not heeded then the consequence is a surprise. If the separation from creation, the planet, continues in the human race, we will be culled. There's no way around it. The system is conscious. The earth is conscious. Everything in creation is endowed with consciousness. Do you really for a moment believe it doesn't know we're the problem? We are at the top of manifest creation in this dimension, but we are expendable. Nothing is bigger than the creation except the creator.

Other races will not interfere in this process. There will be no rescue, and if there was then we would forfeit our autonomy. We would become the wards of another people, another race. Benign races don't want that. The creation was not set up for species daycare. All consequence is paid in full by the party that started the sequence. Karma is a valid universal law. The energy that sustains our reality and all the dual realities above it, the sound and light from the creator, is conscious. Everything is recorded. It's literally impossible to avoid consequence. It can be bartered, transferred, or delayed, just like financial debt, depending on the mood of the lender, but it cannot be forgotten and it cannot be dissolved.

We are responsible for every thought, deed, and action as individuals and as a collective, whether that collective be a family, a community, a nation, a region, or the human race as a whole, and all is set in motion through the universal powers. We get what we ask for, and pretending we didn't understand what we were asking for is not a suitable deferment. This is the way the universe has been set up. We have to be sincere in what we are doing. There's no such thing as being alone, not after what I've experienced.

You're not alone in the world, even when nobody is around you, and you're not alone in your head because there is no *in your head*. Consciousness is a geography, internal and external, and that's just in the worlds that adhere to what we think is time, after those consciousness just is. This is where the extraterrestrials come from, whether they finally appear in a flying disk or walk through a door of light that opens up on your ranch.

Mixed Genetics

Earlier in this chapter I referred to this human race as a hothouse race. The earth is a hothouse, a nursery of sorts. We are not natural creations. We are of mixed extraterrestrial races. This genetic construction applies to the physical and psychic makeup of mankind. The spiritual is the same through all life, whether it be an advanced galactic people like the Andromedan races, who live thousands of years in a single lifetime, or the mineral and insect life on our planet. The spiritual is the same for everything. There is no better or worse, bigger or smaller, richer or poorer. Those qualities only exist as physical and psychic attributes. The mind and access to it is the great divider. An individual mind is an expression of a universal mind. The human race expresses a very low percentage of the universal mind. The mind is a field. It exists external to us but we experience it internally because we have not unified the objective and the subjective yet.

The extraterrestrials stressed that this is not a judgment upon us. Sentient life at the fist level of self-awareness — I think therefore I am — requires time to grow. All growth cycles in the development of a species are long and merciless. The creator allows the process. Limited awareness creates concepts like tragedy in the collective consciousness, but that is just a baby step. At some point in the history of this species we will fly. All species I have dealt with have gone through their developmental generations. These processes take time, a time on scale with the life of a planet, longer even, as many species need to be moved from planets. Movement does not take place in our physical form. It takes place in the sensory body, what some call the astral body.

Many of the scriptures on the planet reference alien races as gods. The blue gods of the Vedics are a race. Shiva is an extraterrestrial. The Abrahamic lineage refers to the Elohim. They too are an extraterrestrial race. The genome on this planet is a protected investment. What it was created for I cannot say because I was not told. Why is anything created? Why do we create children on this planet? The reasons are the same, just on a different scale. Creation for an advanced race is at the level of a new sentient hominid. Creation for us is sons and daughters. Both are done with love and reverence for that which created and allows creation. Everything is a celebration of creation.

The human race is a multicultural experiment. We represent that in our earthly cultures as well. We're not just different in skin color and language — we're different at psychic levels as well, but we are one race, the human race, sharing a collective consciousness, a history, a planet, and a goal of growing into the promise of our creators. We were created to answer questions, to push the narrative of life to new understanding. We are loved. Higher love is not sentimental. It might even seem cold to us. It took me some time to get used to it.

Technology exists in the extraterrestrial races to remediate every problem on earth, air, water, soil, radiation — everything. We do not demonstrate a character where this is likely, though. This is what I meant by cold love. Cosmic law dictates we assume responsibility for ourselves. This does not contradict what I said earlier about increased extraterrestrial contact with human beings. It's just not going to happen at the level of planetary involvement. It will take place in the consciousness of individuals and small groups to foster new ways of thinking and living. The consequences of the choices we have made in the last one hundred and fifty years will not be abated. We will have difficult times to live through.

History of Mankind

We are much older than anthropology, archaeology, and history suggest. The extraterrestrials have not given me a complete history, but there have been many seedings. Each time we repeat the same mistakes and roll back the human race to a remnant population and rebuild. In these rollbacks we lose everything, our history, technology, knowledge, and culture. Creation is not the least bit sentimental. The goal of all life is to close the circle between the creator and the creation, to allow the creator to experience what we experience. This is accomplished by merging the consciousness into the creator. The characteristics of the creator are pushed into the densest dimensions of creation through the sentient life forms that exist there. In a sense, there is no duality. There is only absence. Darkness doesn't exist. There is only an absence of light. Evil doesn't exist. There is only an absence of good. The dualistic composition of our physical, emotional, and mental lives is part of the education sewn into the existence in this very dense dimension in which we live. The higher one goes in consciousness the simpler the creation and its operating principles are. The creation is not here to deceive us. We deceive ourselves.

The last great age of man was Atlantis. It lasted for tens of thousands of years. Everything functioned at higher levels. The technology was equivalent to what we have today but done differently. The foundation was different. It was a human society deemed suitable for planetary coexistence. We had open contact with extraterrestrial races. We developed advanced esoteric knowledge of a spiritual and magical nature. Something went horribly wrong. The Atlanteans attacked the Lemurians and destroyed them, but not before the Lemurians were able to counter strike. It was mutual assured destruction, sheer lunacy, the death wish woven deep into our memory, a pattern we repeat time and time again.

The forces of karma are merciless. We live the same psychodrama over and over again, in small and large scale. Nobody is beyond it. The northern native bands of Canada and the United States degenerated into generations of fighting around the eleventh century. It degenerated into cannibalism and all manner of disrespect for the human being. They were able to pull themselves out of it through the effort of one man, who they called the peacemaker, a prophetic figure in their history. From this came the Iroquois Confederacy, the first expression of interlinked state diplomacy the world had seen, and the model for the republic the United States would become. So much of our growth is based in violence and pain. The case could be made we don't know any other way.

We were also a different being in Atlantis. We had more than two active strands of DNA. We don't really understand DNA yet as a culture. There may be some pockets of understanding in the undisclosed scientific communities that now abound in the world, the bastard offspring on the clandestine Nazi science, but as a people we don't understand DNA yet. DNA is exoteric and esoteric. It operates in several dimensions at once, what spiritual language might call the astral and the causal dimensions atop the physical. Encoded in DNA is ancestral memory, cellular memory, and the unmanifest events of a new life, hard as this is to believe.

Free will is an illusion that happens as a result of our limited consciousness while alive. It doesn't really exist, or, rather it exists but it's not what we think it is. It more comes down to a simple binary decision — forgive or collect. It's no accident that our spiritual teachings on this planet focus on debt and forgiveness. If the collections of karma are not made then the lessons risk being lost, but, at the same time, forgiveness allows the practitioner to gain new spiritual equity, new liberation from the clumsy cycles human beings create, and more grace. Many times when a human being is possessed by the spirit of retribution there is a blindness that comes about. Once the retribution is enacted, there is a return to clarity, and they are as horrified by what they have done as anybody else. They understand what they have done, the madness and inhumanity of it, and the act of forgiveness can bring spiritual equity to all parties.

Our most esoteric spiritual teachings are carried over from Atlantis. They had a different base for their technology and it was more focused on consciousness. They understood many things. Their knowledge was carried over in Sumer. This is the longest lasting post-flood human civilization. It persisted with one language and culture. The Atlantean culture persisted in some forms in Sumer, including the remnant of extraterrestrial contact. They had technology and metaphysical under-standings not openly understood today.

The Atlantean secrets migrated from the demise of Sumer to the birth of Babylon, where they were preserved in enough measure to pass on what would become the Egyptian religions, their relics sought all over the world to this day, and from Egypt there is a kind of knowledge-diaspora. From here it moves into Greece and Rome, and from Rome into Europe and Byzantium, and into the Middle-East, but not since Sumer has it been public. It has been preserved in secret doctrines in secret societies. It is a metaphysical geography which understands the energy of the planet, the grid lines, and the portals, like the ones on my property. They understand the transdimensionality of our species.

My Contact

Once you are contacted by extraterrestrials they never leave you. They become tied to your life in a mysterious way. Just when you forget about them they reappear. Sometimes the appearance can be quite dra-matic. They manifest right in front of you. It's hard to explain. It's dif-ferent than the grays appearing, which still happens from time to time, but they have stopped all harassment. The benign extraterrestrials are simply not there one moment and there the next. There is no process of materialization.

People ask me to describe them. They could easily pass as human, but, at the same time, there's something very distinct about them. They seem too perfect in some ways, like Hollywood people, the hair and teeth, the physical bearing, all of it makes them stand out. If you were in a conference room at a hotel, you would notice them among hun-dreds of other people, but not in such a way that you'd know they're not of this world. You'd just register something distinct.

I wouldn't call them warm, not the way we describe warm. They don't indulge their emotions the way we do. Everything just is. They seem to be operating from this perspective that transcends the fallacy of free will. They know what the correct thing to do is in any situation based on the creational laws, and they don't deviate. It gives them a kind of mechanical countenance. The energy around them is positive. It's not unpleasant to deal with them, just different, not human. All of their words are spoken with extreme care in their selection. It just is sums it up fairly well.

They crossed my life through Brandy Howe, and in that crossing they continue to present themselves. In some ways they seem distant. From my perspective we're talking about the future of the human race, our planet, it's environment, and critical things. When they speak back it's like they're explaining the warranty on a new car — very matter of fact. Nothing seems to rile them. Their emotional constitution seems vastly different than ours. I don't want to characterize them as insensitive. They are anything but insensitive. They can feel and intuit what I want to talk about before it forms in my mind. It's just the complete and total absence of any kind of reactive nature. Everything just is. God help you if you react to anything with what I would describe as the human sense of how things operate, which they regard as childish and entitled. They do not tolerate it well at all. Interacting with them has taught me a new sense of decorum.

Chapter 19

The Crossroad

The human race is at a crossroads. We have done as much as we can with our technological paradigm. We've been on a *boom boom* economy for more than a century, where boom is the explosion of gasoline igniting in a chamber. The last one hundred and twenty years can be defined by three main things — electrical illumination at night, rapid transport (at least faster than horse or walking), and disembodied voice. Aside from this not much has happened.

A lot of the ancillary deficits have been enormous as well, but nobody is really keeping track of that. There is no missing consciousness social science in the academic world, no minister of consciousness at the governmental level, or so it seems upon first glance. It's a curious oddity that the things least talked about in public society are the things most talked about in secret societies.

Consciousness is the most studied thing in the intelligence world. It doesn't seem that way because we're not explicitly told, however, we are tacitly told all the time, and here we come once again to the military-industrial-entertainment complex, the latter being music and movies, which have been the largest fabricator of global consciousness. It's here we're allowed to entertain all notions of imagination, talking to animals, going into space, the nature of time, and the nature of consciousness.

It's become stock in these farces to portray the hero as imbalanced for entertaining premodern realities, whether it be Indiana Jones explaining to us through his exploits in *Raiders of the Lost Ark* that the Nazi regime was very much involved in premodern culture, the esoteric, the magical, and any manner of things we can enjoy in a movie cinema and regard as silly superstition the moment we leave the cinema, or Christopher Nolan showing us the idea of planting an idea in someone's mind while they sleep, or hacking someone's mind in his film *Inception*.

We laugh it off the moment we leave the cinema. The truth is the intelligence world is heavily focused on the occult, and it always has been, even way before the time John Dee entertained the British Monarchy as the court sorcerer. Nor can we assume for a moment that institutions like the Vatican are unaware, either. They are another early pioneer of the intelligence world, with each and every archdiocese operating as an embassy, and what do embassies have? They have ambassadors for relationship maintenance, trade delegates to expand commercial interests, and spies. That triumvirate has been as consistent for the last millennia as light, transport, and disembodied voice have been to the last one hundred years. It couldn't be that Spielberg and Nolan are telling us a truth in their films. No, of course not. Yet they are. They are not telling us *the* truth to the last detail, instead they are telling us *a* truth.

We forget how new the thought bubble we live in is. It's less than one hundred and fifty years old. It begins with three things — light, transportation, and disembodied voice.

Light

The illumination of cities really cannot be understated. Wabash, Indiana was the first town to introduce electric street lights in the United States. That was in 1880. The effect of this was staggering. Commerce could now operate twenty-four hours a day. The old gas lamps that fueled the whaling industry were sufficient to keep busy streets illuminated at night in London and other European locales, but they were no match for the productivity boom that electrical illumination would bring.

Illumination changed everything. As it spread into the larger cities it fueled a night culture. Night had been a highly underutilized part of the day for the human race. We had lived much more within the circadian rhythm of the planet. People worked on the land, and they went to bed early and rose early. It was a natural cycle. Illumination broke that cycle. More and more people began to work at night. Businesses that could continue their revenue streams at night did so. Most importantly, we began to generate our own electrical fields. Not much attention has been paid to this, at least not in the public space. Electrical fields have had a very profound effect on human beings. We ourselves are electrical beings. Illumination at night produced a lot of intellectual work that could be done. All that was required was a light and a desk.

Not much has changed with the electrical system we put in over a century ago. What we have not done as a species is take stock of what this changes brought about. It begins simply enough with illumination and cities, but other changes were made to human existence. People don't make the connections. It was also the very first monthly bill. Of course there were other monies owed. Many farms were under mortgage if they were not family-owned, but family owned land was a big part of the American landscape. It is safe to say that the electrical bill was the first monthly bill introduced into modern society. If you wanted to enjoy this other part of the day, the night, you had to pay. The electrical system that we chose, the AC/DC system, was specifically selected for its ability to generate revenue and be measured on a meter, which produced the monthly bill. The month is a lunar cycle, like women's menstruation, so it seems natural. A great effort has been made to *mimic* the natural world in the modern and post-modern worlds.

If you look at the average household now in the early twenty-first century there is a laundry list of monthly bills — mortgage or rent, electricity, gas or fuel, home insurance, life insurance, phone bill, data usage for phone, sports and music lessons for children, school fees, daycare, groceries, public transportation monthly pass (train or bus), parking, cable television, and the list could go on almost ad nausea. You get the point. The electrical bill started it all, and now we live in perpetually illuminated cities, even the daytime is illuminated now with digital billboards, and the unnatural cycle we follow in bills, all matched to the moon's cycle — monthly. Our fiscal year follows the seasons, four seasons matched to four quarters in the markets, all a mimicry of the harvest.

Rapid Transport

The next big push forward was the combustion engine. This took away the necessity of horsepower in a very short period of time. The coal fired steam engine had been around for passenger trains, but the autonomy and independence of the personal automobile was a major step forward in the ability of human beings to move freely on the planet.

The combustion engine was just the beginning. The first major breakthrough comes with an American named Henry Ford. He created something astounding. He created the first factory and the first assembly line. The assembly line parted work into various units or tasks and guaranteed the production time of a completed unit. It was a major step forward for industry and a major step backward for human ingenuity and creativity. I characterize it as a step backward for human ingenuity and creativity because human beings are no longer required to create something.

Manufacturing something and creating something are far different. Just take a moment and think of all the people you've seen interviewed in the last twenty-five years, all of the people who are smiling and happy, the chief executive officers of large corporations, the Hollywood actors, the inventors and successful entrepreneurs, are all part of the creative class. Creative people are the happiest people on the planet. This is because of the fundamental truth that man is a creative being. When a human being is creative they are literally commiserating with the creator. This is a very important point to understand, and it's one of the things that separates us from extremely advanced extraterrestrial races.

Prior to industrialization, human beings participated in their cultures and their cultures were the main repository of their creativity. Native storytelling in ritual was the height of human expression. In context of the world we've created in the twenty-first century what I'm saying seems ridiculous, but stay with me. In the end you will be rewarded with an epiphany, which, in classical parlance, means the sudden appearance of a god, and, in modern parlance, a sudden change of consciousness. What Henry Ford did was guarantee a material living for people who manufactured. All promise of a creative life was forfeited by those who went into the manufacturing sector.

With the ability to move vast distances in a short period of time, human beings began to grow in new ways. Anyone with a car could take off and see vast swatches of their country, something which had not been possible in centuries previous. Most people lived a localized life, a kind of village life or tribal life minus the actual native culture. When we began to move around we begin to encounter people who are not like us.

From this ability to move around comes another expansion of our commercial expression. Things had always been traded by boat and by train, but the distribution points were extremely limited. With the advent of the combustion engine and the automobile made cheaper through the manufacturing process of Henry Ford, radical transformations to our society comes about. From the combustion engine comes the oil economy.

The first dynasties in America where banking and oil. Prior to them people could gain notoriety and wealth through massive farm operations, but nothing approximating what was achievable through the centralized command of corporations and the distribution power of the combustion engine. The trucking industry began. In one generation we have a figure in Jimmy Hoffa who comes to rival the power of the President of the United States simply by being the leader of the Teamsters Union which controls all trucking in America.

From this point onward we get the great standoff between labor and capital, which remains fundamentally unresolved until corporations successfully lobby government to commence free trade, culminating in the Free Trade agreement between Canada and the US, coincidentally around the time the Berlin Wall was coming down, which had *forced* economic cooperation between nations — economy of scale being the common denominator.

The purpose of free trade from the corporate perspective was to allow companies to increase profits by seeking out labor at pennies on the dollar compared to what the unions had driven the labor costs up to in North America. We also get a further commingling of the human race. Prior to free trade and international commerce there really wasn't a lot of interaction between human civilizations except through colonization, which was practiced mainly by the British with ancillary roles played by the French, the Portuguese, and the Spanish, with the Vatican operating as the godfather — *el padrino*.

Disembodied Voice

The first example of the projected voice is the radio. The radio comes about as a household appliance in the early twentieth century. Only the voice is projected. Families used to sit around on a Saturday night and listen to a broadcast from a centralized location. This was the beginning of a new form of culture as well, the beginning of a digital culture. The characteristics of a digital culture are profoundly different from the characteristics of a community. Of course the first radios were not digital as we use the word now. They were analog. Digital is just the word I choose to encompass the idea of disembodied voices. This new culture allowed people to participate in cultures larger than their community. This radically changed human consciousness, whether we realize it or not.

From the radio we move to the telephone. The telephone precedes the radio but I place radio more prominently in my thesis because no wires were needed. It was voice liberated from the clumsy poles and wires telephones required, like a nervous system minus the body. Suddenly commerce changes dramatically. You can communicate over vast geography without getting on a steam ship or using carrier pigeons. The movement of the disembodied voice into two-way private communication through telephones changed everything, and it extended the utility of electricity which brought the nighttime illumination. They started to work in concert, the disembodied voices, the nighttime illumination, and the rapid transportation.

The disembodied voice becomes the disembodied person when film comes about, at first, rather comically if you consider it, minus the voice. The first films were silent films. They had to figure out how to combine the voice and the picture, but that didn't take too long. Then the transportation moved into the transport of the voice and the form as it appeared in real life, a perfect two-dimensional replication of the human experience as it came through our senses, and what did we populate talking pictures with — the imagination we officially left in the premodern era. The only problem with this is that the human experience, the inner and outer human being, were separated. In the past they had been unified. That's what people are looking for when they go to Peru to do ayahuasca, the unification of the inner and outer person.

It's interesting to note that many people who have tried ayahuasca

speak about meeting extraterrestrials, seeing flying saucers, and interacting with non-human beings, a lot like my ranch. How do we know
about ayahuasca? The plants spoke to the natives and revealed themselves. The speaking with the plants the natives refer to is in dreams,
but the things revealed to them are of the world, scientifically and precisely of the world, a union of the inner and the outer, the whole man
understanding nature. Please do not confuse my example with an en-
dorsement of ayahuasca. There are many ways to understand the inner
and the outer as the whole being, and ayahuasca was developed for native cultures, not for recreational spiritualists from the West who abuse
it.

From film we move to computers and the advent of the true digital
age, where a two-dimensional representation of voice and picture can
be used any time with video calling. Then they packaged it all in hand-
held devices, but the same trinity persists — illumination, transport,
and disembodied voice, all the things premodern societies had in their
imaginations.

The Trinity of the Modern and Post-Modern

These three things — electrical illumination, rapid transportation, and
disembodied voices — form the trinity of the modern and the postmod-
ern age. Nothing we've done has really changed this principle trinity
which is responsible for the massive social and cultural change the human race has gone through. We are no longer a genuine culture. In the
quiet and stillness of the past age we articulated a relationship with the
fourth dimension. It comes through in our folklore, our mythologies,
our superstitions, and our spiritual culture, where spiritual just means
knowledge of self outside of the body. It doesn't mean the individual
consciousness has migrated all the way back to its source.

In his work at Harvard, John Mack equates the abduction phenomenon
with religious and spiritual experience, which he notes seems to end as
a cultural phenomenon around the beginning of the Industrial Age. It's
an interesting observation by Mack. Experiences which were participa-
tory in the past become part of the observational sciences of the emerging Western consciousness — anthropology, history, archaeology, so-
ciology, and psychiatry. The entirety of human consciousness gets hi-
jacked at the end of the nineteenth century, gone is the wistful interre-

lationship with imagination that marked premodern civilizations. It's all brain health, lobes in the brain, electrical impulses, and pharmacology, the absence of imagination being a very lucrative economy. That's the official public narrative, anyway.

The only person allowed to speak as an expert in the area of human consciousness in a court of law is a psychiatrist. Are we then saying they are the repository of all knowledge about human consciousness? They have the power to administer custodial incarceration to an individual. Yet, much like the electrical engineer who can't tell you what electricity is, psychiatry can't tell us what schizophrenia is, but they are convinced the voices in the afflicted's heads are auditory hallucinations. It certainly can't be, as Jerry Marzinsky states, that they are possessed. That would align consciousness with more than one dimension, and the name of the game from the inception of the modern age has been to flatten human consciousness to one reality, this three-dimensional reality, and it has been done intentionally in full knowledge that man is a multidimensional being.

As the modern world began to take shape new organizational principles came into being. The automobile necessitated oil, roads, and street lights. Somebody had to pay for it. They created banking and formed the US Federal Reserve in 1913, and the sixteenth amendment made income tax legal in the same year, 1913. The government created a bank to borrow money from on behalf of the people, who, in a sense, are cosigners on the borrowing. A citizen became a partner, a partner with liability. The modern age is trying to sweep man's trans-dimensional nature under the carpet. They want a neat package now that isolates a human being from spiritual identity. This is how we are controlled. The only question remaining is who or what is controlling us?

Consent

The most important thing to understand is that we went from a poetic culture to a literal culture. When we turned our backs on imagination we shut a door in ourselves, a door that goes back to the source of creation. Creation was finished the moment it began because it happened outside of time and space. This means the parts of creation we can't see with our eyes we see with our imagination. Everything documented in creation through our myths and fables is fundamentally true. This does mot mean literally true. It means that the mythologies when contemplated upon render a truth.

One of the biggest casualties of the death of imagination is God. Religion has always been the repository of the imagination. The famous Irish writer James Joyce was uncannily accurate in his first novel, *Portrait of the Artist as a Young Man* when he gave up his birth religion of Catholicism to become, as his central character Stephan Dedalus put it, *a priest of the imagination.* Joyce did not give up on the imagination as the doorway to God, he rejected the control of the imagination the priests had. He wanted to know for himself, not take someone else's word for it.

The death of the imagination is spiritual death while alive, and spiritual death has many characteristics — illness, mental instability, breach of consciousness, (read possession and occupation here). Have you noticed the explosion of horror movies featuring possession — the *Paranormal Activity* franchise (six installments with a seventh scheduled for 2021), the *Insidious* franchise (four installments so far), *The Nun*, and too many more to list here. One could make the case we're fascinated by possession. It's a symptom of the death of imagination.

In nature all thing are preyed upon. Almost everything created controls the population of something else in creation. We see this in the water, on the land, and in the air. Nothing in nature is safe from predation except the top predators in any given ecosystem. In the rainforests of Central America the jaguar is atop the cycle of predation, but, like any top predator they are susceptible to any failures in the ecosystem. If the salmon stocks fail in northern Canada then the bears run the risk of starving. The populations of top predators in their ecosystem is dependent on the maintenance of the ecosystem, what we might call the liability of kings.

We started observing culture at the beginning of the Industrial Revolution. Before that, culture was participated in, not observed. The imagination was lived, not discarded. The seminal work that commenced the field of anthropology was *The Golden Bough: A Study in Magic and Religion*, by Sir James George Frazer, a knighted Scotsman. The book is a comparative study of religion and mythology, a brilliant foundation for the emerging science of anthropology. It was published in 1890, again curiously centered in this emerging objective culture of the Industrial Revolution.

Frazer postulated that man moves through three stages — magic, religion, then science. In magical thinking, the culture is attempting to directly control the forces of nature through magical rituals. The succession of kings was a magical ritual in Frazer's work, the death and resurrection of the king was an unconscious metaphor for the setting and rising of the sun, and for the natural rhythm of seasons. In his first edition he included Christ in this metaphor of the resurrecting of a king. It was scandalous at the time.

In religious thinking the human population petitions an intermediary to control the forces of nature. In scientific thinking we believe we can control the forces of nature, but a quick look at the state of the world nullifies this assertion. Nature is furious with us. Religion has become the most resilient aspect of the imagination, a kind of lone survivor of the Industrial and Technological Revolutions. They collectively participated in the murder of paganism, deeming their religions superior to the tribal *superstitions* that preceded them. Religion has always been the only institutionalized form of imagination, the only form of imagination to register, get licenses, tax waivers, and be officially sanctioned in the industrial and technological ages. Religion represents the institutionalized imagination. The problem is the imagination cannot be institutionalized, nor can love or compassion. These are uniquely human characteristics.

Institutional compassion is the biggest lie ever told to the human race. Compassion can only be given by a living being. I say living being because it's not just human beings that can demonstrate compassion. Other evolved mammals on earth can show compassion. So what happens when we institutionalize everything, education, social benefits, child protective services, correctional services through prisons, drug and alcohol rehabilitation, and the myriad codes, statutes, and acts that govern the flow of commerce? Nothing happens. The intended correction never occurs. The growth into imagination never occurs. So why do we do it in the first place? How did we become so detached from ourselves, so distant from a true human experience, so subservient to the cult of expertise? We were tricked into giving our consent is the simplest possible answer. Nothing can happen without consent.

Reptilians, Black Magic and Satanism

You may be wondering why in a book about an alien infested ranch with portals I'm talking about labor, capital, the late nineteenth century, twentieth century, the early twenty-first century, the institutionalization of the human race, the co-opting of all land on the planet into a fiduciary system, and science. Fundamentally these are realizations that have come about based on my encounters with extraterrestrials. You see when you consider extraterrestrials you must think of the human race as a species. Gone are all the divisions that have haunted us in the past, the Protestants and Catholics in Northern Ireland, the Israelis and the Palestinians, the rich and the poor, black and white, big and small. All of it goes away when you begin interacting with extraterrestrials. Only one question remains. What ails this species? The human race.

I touched upon predation in nature. The reason I did that is to point out that predation does not stop at the physical dimension. Through our senses and our mind we are at the top of creation. Nothing really preys upon us. From time to time we read a story about somebody being mauled by a black bear in Northern Canada, or attacked by a mountain lion in California, or bitten by a shark in the Pacific Ocean, but these things are extremely rare and it's safe to say that the human race is beyond predation. But are we? When we open up to the next dimension, the fourth dimension, where most of the extraterrestrial contact comes from, a new landscape of predation emerges. Human beings produce *things* that are of value to other species.

I also spoke about creation being finished because it took place outside of time and space. That means that nobody really discovers anything, that a human consciousness either wanders into a new geography of imagination and sees something, either in a dream or a vision, and then feverishly works on producing it in the world, or it is given by a fourth dimensional being. This has been the history of the human race as we go through this rapid period of invention and scientific innovation. We've gone from outhouses and pasturing animals to space travel and a fully integrated world through the Internet in a century and a half. More has happened in the last one hundred and fifty years than in the last one thousand years.

The question that remains is where did all this innovation come from? The answer is that most of it is given to us. If linear processes revealed everything in the worlds then we would master a linear process to reveal the entire universe to us. No such linear process has come about. The transmission of information from its inception to the general population can generally be done in a literal process. Our education system is a linear process. Children begin in kindergarten at five years of age and go on until whenever they stop, some people getting multiple doctoral degrees. The effect of all this linear process is the nullification of the creative process. The mind is a tremendous mimic. If you put human consciousness into a twenty year cycle of linear processes then consciousness will assume the modality of linear processes. In the transference of information we forfeit the creativity at the individual level.

In understanding who is giving us information we have to understand the multi-dimensional reality in which we live. We've already discussed that most of the native mythologies go back to star seedings. The Navajo people of the American southwest talk about coming through portals to this planet. Here we get to the greatest duality of my story, the duality of predation at transdimensional level and the duality of self-interest and service to creation and the Creator. It's important also to note at this point that the word extraterrestrial, by the etymology alone, encompasses everything not of the earth that engages with human beings as individuated forms. Not many people consider how that includes all of the angels and demons and all of the gods that are populated in our religions. The actual creator of this transdimensional reality is not an individuated form as we understand beings and entities. The attribution of human qualities to the angels cannot be overlooked. They are extraterrestrial. They are not of the earth but they are individuated beings. They even have names, like the Archangel Michael and the Archangel Gabriel. Even the gods we worship have names.

Our world has been influenced by and inadvertently governed by forces darker than you can imagine. This is by far the most difficult part of the story to tell. Much of this has been related to me through my contact with growth centered extraterrestrials. I use the term *growth centered* because benign seems a little bit too personal. There's nothing really personal with the extraterrestrials. They don't want karmic entanglement with our species. It gives them a standoffish attitude that at first I regarded as aloofness. As I evolved through my engagements with them I understood better why they choose the protocols they do.

A growth centered extraterrestrial race is interested in the well-being of all things. It's the same thing as a loving human being. However, the human being while alive will be more personally engaged in the lives of other human beings — spouse, children, extended family, close friends, and things like this. These are karmic relationships. The extraterrestrials don't have karma with our species. A grave circumstance that you could imagine, like an earthquake that could kill hundreds of millions of people, elicits no emotional response from the extraterrestrials. Being human we register this as cold, but they follow a law that is higher, from millions of years of mnemonic understanding of galaxies, life, growth, species, and it creates a disposition where the very notion of tragedy is spiritual pornography. They see things within incarnational patterns, ages of our species forgotten to our history, lost in time to us, but not to them. They have the ability to read the records of time and creation. The minutest details of our existence on this planet and other planets is known to them. They don't get emotional.

The human race has been in symbiotic relationships with negative extraterrestrials for millennia, mainly reptilians from the Draco star system, however they're not the only ones. The reptilians go by many names in human history. The Chinese and Japanese have dragon mythology. The Egyptian Book of the Dead speaks of the alligator people. Their drawings appear in temples and pyramids. The Islamic culture makes reference to Jin appearing in either human or serpent form, and the serpent in the Garden of Eden. The reptilians and a collection of self-serving races from the the Orion sector have had a profound impact on human history and development. They are the basis of the Luciferian rebellion story. Many of our stories are true. We just have difficulty as a species mapping the mythological to the literal. It's part of the veil between our three-dimensional reality and the fourth dimension.

The laws of creation are clear for all, and most races don't break them. It's not out of any respect for the creational process, but more by an understanding that breach of the law brings consequence. The law of free will is is understood by human beings, though it is often broken. A human being is held to be sovereign, as are all sentient beings. However, the art of breaching free will is manufacturing consent. Nothing dictates that a bi-dimensional species like the reptilians cannot contract with a one dimensional species like human beings on earth. The contracts never work out well for us. Absent context we lack the sophistry to make a good deal. If this all sounds a lot like fable, myth, or literature, it's because it is. It is the contract with the devil, the Faustian bargain. It's all real, only substitute the literary and mythological figures of the stories and scriptures with the reptilians and you've gone from fable to fact. It's that simple.

Reptilians are a fourth dimensional species that can engage human beings through mediums, psychics, ritual, and sacrifice. They can also possess and occupy a living human being, and they have been running a hybrid incarnation program on planet earth for some time. Most of the powerful people on the planet are reptilian, whether they be in government or business or entertainment. The reptilians love to live among us as venerated figures. Absent meaningful relationship with the creation or the creator, they draw their energy from us, and from other mammalian species like us in this and nearby galaxies.

Whenever you see something lacking all humanity on the planet it's reptilian. It's really been right in front of us the whole time. We dress it up as something else — psychopathology, sociopaths — but the thing they have in common is the ability to appear human with no humanity, and what better to act with no humanity than something which is not human. The reptilians are responsible for wars in this and neighboring galaxies that have lasted hundreds of thousands of years. A truce has existed for some time but the Draco Reptilians in particular find ways to blur the lines, one of which is us, the human beings on planet earth. It gets worse.

There is no spiritual figure called Satan. It's just another aspect of the confusion surrounding mankind's inability to reconcile the mythological with the literal. It doesn't help that a race of beings governing and manipulating us creates bi-dimensional narratives to confound and confuse people of religious sincerity. Here we arrive at one of the moments where I reacted in front of the positive extraterrestrials who explained things to me — *How could you allow this to go on!* They weren't impressed or moved. That's why I describe them as distant. They're like gods watching from above as we find fire and invent the wheel, knowing the eons it will take us to realize our multidimensional nature, our connection with creation and the creator, and the whole thing is completely natural, including being preyed upon by a fourth dimensional race of scaled hominids.

The perspective on the extraterrestrials who helped me understand my ranch? It's a natural part of our growth cycle. We got ourselves into it and we need to get ourselves out of it. They do get involved. The very fact that they're communicating with me and other people on the planet is evidence of that, but it's an advisory role.

I got the feeling dealing with the extraterrestrials that we human beings were a proxy war, that we were being used by them and the regressive extraterrestrials, like the reptilians and the rogue grays that terrorized my ranch, as a battle between themselves through us, the way we saw the United States and the Soviet Union fought in Vietnam and other countries. Sadly though, it's darker and more pathetic than this. Our main problem is not the reptilians. It's the human beings who contract with them, who bite the apple for want of the forbidden knowledge.

To understand what is happening on planet earth, you must understand the dimensional nature of existence. Consciousness is actually spread across multiple dimensions. The majority of our experience is concentrated in the densest dimension, our physical reality on this planet. At the next level, the fourth dimension, we have been an occupied species for some time. It's part of the limited consciousness of the human race that we can't conceptualize an alien invasion as anything other than physical. This is not the case. We are occupied at the fourth dimension. Where this story goes now is not for the faint of heart.

There's no way for me to explain the situation except by giving you a very clear example of what I mean. When nation states throughout history have warred with each other it has been for resources. Here on the physical plane resource means physical wealth like land and water and minerals and human beings for slavery. This is a very simple concept to understand. We all live in this dimension. Living in this Dimension we can understand what conquest and profiting from that conquest is, but what is being sought when we're dealing with a species that is fully bi-dimensional like the reptilians? If they exist largely in the fourth dimension with a limited presence in our three-dimensional reality what is it that they're looking for? What is the plunder? It's us. We're the plunder, but not in the limited sense of slavery.

Creation has endowed this human race with special qualities. I've already told you that we are the product of multiple species in this universe. Human beings possess the genetics of multiple extraterrestrial races. In a sense, we are an experiment. We were over this material in the previous chapter. This race, the human race on planet earth, has been given a very special gift. The ability to know the Creator, to hold the Creator in our consciousness. Everything in creation seeks the Creator, but many of the species that have been in existence for millions of years have made mistakes so severe that they have lost their path back to the Creator.

The main mistake that has been made is self augmentation through technology. We ourselves are right at that point now. Transhumanism is right around the corner. More to the point, we are a delicacy on the fourth dimension. The richness of our emotional constitution produces the equivalent of tastes for other species on the fourth Dimension. Just as we can enjoy the taste of chocolate here on Earth, these other species, especially the reptilians, savor our emotional taste and energy on the fourth dimension. For lack of a better way of putting it, it's the closest they can get to the Creator.

The situation became so severe in a later twentieth century that those who could see it might have compared the fourth dimension or at least the lower fourth dimension to a by dimensional crack house full of addicted species feeding off the human race. The reptilians are literally addicted to us the way human beings can become addicted to crystal meth or crack or heroin. The ingestion of the human energy is different. Before we get to that, I need to explain a few other things.

Part of cosmic law dictates that there must be a disclosure. We discuss this in other parts of the book. I've already told you how Hollywood is part of a disclosure mechanism about what's going on in the fourth dimension. Disclosure is a cosmic law. Nothing in creation exists outside of the law. The name of the game is to get the consent of the person or species that you want to interact with. The game that the reptilians have been playing is miscontextualized consent. In a sense, many of our religions are disclosure mechanisms. Satan was invented to represent this fourth-dimensional conundrum. If we behave a certain way, the reptilians do not become a problem. They are a feeding species and they feed off of our lower emotions, our anger, our rage, our frustration, our sadness, our tears are like wine to them. We get disclosure of this in the form of our religions. The Catholic Church and the present Vatican is the most reptilian-centric organization on the planet right now. Take a look at the Hall of the Pontifical Audiences in Rome, then take a look at the sculpture that sits right behind where the pope sits. All of these image are available on the Internet. Can you see the serpent in the roof design? Can you see suffering humanity in the sculpture? Now, many Catholics still under the spell might see this as symbolic of the struggle against the serpent in the garden, but why represent that in the architecture? Why not something more triumphant? Why not something representative of God's love? The Vatican is completely and utterly a reptilian institution now. It's important to understand that as part of the *required* disclosure to which even the extraterrestrials are beholden — we must be told, but how we are told, whether it be on the six o'clock news, or through a scripture or mythology, is inconsequential — we have been told.

The characteristics of reptilian culture are horror, terror, rape, murder, pedophilia, and the chemical harvesting of the human body that has been terrorized. This is how they enjoy the energies of the human being. We are consumed and ingested just as we consume the mammals that we eat on planet earth, but we don't eat meat for a high. We eat it for sustenance and for protein. The reptilians consume us for a particular energy we produce that is like a narcotic to them. This energy is produced in us at the base of the spine.

It goes by many names already spoken of in this book — chi, prani, ether, or orgone, to name a few — and it is stolen through rape, specifically sodomy, and the energy is particularly undiluted in children, and, specifically in prepubescent boys. This explains the epidemic of pedophilia in the world now, specifically in the West. It's practiced heavily in the Catholic Church, certain sects of Judaism, among the Free Masons, and other secret societies.

It's interesting to note that during the 2016 presidential run, at the traditional preelection archdiocese dinner in New York City, then candidate Trump alluded to missing children in Haiti. It was an uncomfortable moment for Hillary Clinton in the audience. Pedophilia raised its head again in the run up to the election in the form of Pizzagate, which the media was quick to label a conspiracy theory. Hillary's campaign manager, John Podesta, was the most talked about figure tied to pedophilia. It was enough for him to lay low for a few months. Podesta has tweeted numerous times about *disclosure*, which has come to be the catchphrase for governments revealing *secret* information on UFOs and extraterrestrials.

There's a whole subculture involved in this now, with television shows like *Ancient Aliens*, but I can assure you what they are giving is allowable portions of the truth, and they are only doing this now because the topic has built up such a presence in the collective unconscious, the *spiritus mundi* that they have no choice. Many of the powerful in the world have joined reptilian culture already. It's human corollary is Satanism. As I said already, there is no Satan. Satanism is the ritual culture given to humanity by the reptilians. It steals the energies the reptilians want. Many of the human practitioners are possessed by reptilians in the fourth dimension, again, what we call in in classical esoteric or occult terminology the astral plane.

We spoke earlier in this book about ancient knowledge brought forward from Atlantis. The knowledge I speak of is the knowledge that was given to me living on my ranch in Rainbow Valley. The earth has a series of electromagnetic anomalies, or portals, that allow entities and beings from other dimensions to visit the Earth. These other dimensions are completely real as I have demonstrated in my story. The knowledge carried forward from Atlantis is the knowledge of the gridlines and the portals on the planet. When you see war going on in the world there are only a few possible reasons for it. It can be for a physical resource for monetary control, and here oil comes to mind, or it is a war for ancient artifacts that explain the past or an existing portal.

The ultimate irony of our age is that at the public level we believe that we are ruled by reason, objectivity, and science. Nothing could be further from the truth. We are ruled by black magic. Along with the portals, the rulers of this world hold an ancient knowledge of magic and ritual. As difficult as this is for people to believe, I assure you magic is real and it influences everything on this planet. The Germans were the first to build spacecraft on earth. They did this during World War II. For those who cannot reconcile science and magic, ask yourselves this: why did such a scientifically advanced people like the Germans entertain rituals, an obsession with the occult, ancient artifacts, and ritual magic? The answer is because the two things go together. It has to do with the subjective — human interior and imagination — and the objective — the world of tangible reality.

In his work *Fear and Loathing in Las Vegas*, the writer Hunter S Thompson gives us one the first public reference to adrenochrome, a drug produced by the adrenal gland, and made richer for the participant by putting the victim it is harvested from through absolute terror prior to harvest, which kills the human producer. It is a drug revered by the Satanic elite, both for its effects and its procurement. The effect is bi-dimensional consciousness in a degree far greater than any of the natural psychedelics, including ayahuasca. The procurement kills the human being in a pageant of terror and violence, fulfilling the Satanic edict of desecrating the human being. Do you see how it all goes together now? There is no Satan. The hatred for humanity attributed to this mythical figure is a cover story for inter-species contempt — human and reptilian — and the bi-dimensional nature of the reptilians, though they can appear on the earth and many of them live here now in human form, which means their physical form is human, achieved either through a hybrid birthing program, like the one described in this book that produced Cynthia Crawford, and remember, she goes as far back as the OSS days, so imagine what they can do today, or a human being is possessed by a reptilian.

Now we can sum up the situation. All of the science and systems we have developed and brought into the world since the the late nineteenth century are flawed, and what's more, they are deliberately flawed. This includes the social sciences, the medical sciences, the hard sciences, and the systems of governance that have evolved. All of them have been constructed to murder the human imagination, which is the human spirit in a diluted form. It's no accident that all the truths of the premodern world have been erased. It's no accident that we have been incapacitated and reduced to spiritual infancy. It's been done so we don't see what's going on around us. It's a herd mentality as they coral us into cities with Agenda 2030, reinforced with all the bad energy through the cell towers and the electromagnetic poison, and all of it done deliberately to bring this race to its knees. You see, we are not waiting for the Hollywood version of invasion where ships appear over cities, the aliens are visible to everyone, and its some version of a heroic journey. We have already been colonized.

In 1996 I moved onto Stardust Ranch. I don't know if things always happen for a reason. I believe they do. After twenty-three years of living with portals and alien visitation, both hostile and non-hostile, I now have to share what I know with the world. I'm John Edmonds and this is my story, and my story, as individual and uncommon as it is, became the story of us all. It has taken me this long to get my story out. I couldn't tell it myself. I had to find someone I could trust. That happened in 2012 when I met Bruce MacDonald, but it took this long to tell the story. I pray it finds the hearts and minds who can awaken the divine imagination to counter what has happened to the human race. We are magnificent and beautiful beings, and our story is far from over however bleak it may look. We hold the solutions to every problem within us, and we will find our way to the majesty predestined in our species, of this I have faith.

Part VI

Afterword

My name is Joyce Edmonds. I've been around for this whole story. It's true that I did not want to move to Stardust Ranch in 1996. I had a bad feeling about the place from the moment that I saw it. We were the only ones in Rainbow Valley in 1996. The place felt very creepy to me. I did not like being at the ranch alone. In the early years I did not know how to explain what I felt. I think sometimes it came across to my husband, John, as perhaps just a woman's issue. I didn't want to go outside the ranch at night.

When things started happening at the ranch I was in denial for a long time. Most of the weird and violent stuff happened to John first. My coping mechanism was to deny it was happening. Over time I realized that I was just using John for my own denial. It became clear to me that the things happening at night were happening to both of us. It's hard to give a word to how I felt about this. I could say horror, but it doesn't quite capture everything. There really is no word. I guess I will have to stay with horror.

My earliest understanding that something was not right had to do with waking up in the morning and having marks on my body. My earliest encounters with whatever we have in the house were not visual. For me it started by hearing things. The things made certain noises. The grays make a hissing sound. I would also hear things moving around at night. I can remember very clearly the exact incident that took all of my denial away. John and I woke up in the morning and both of us were extremely raw and chafed on the inside of our thighs. We figured out that we had been abducted.

It was horrifying for me. After that things proceeded to the point where I was being taken multiple times. I don't really have a full recollection of it. However, I was waking up at different times in the middle of the night. It was usually between two and three-thirty in the morning. I would hear a lot of things, and sometimes when I woke up the whole bedroom was lit up. It was always a machine sound. I can't quite describe it. It wasn't mechanical like a factory sound. Machine sound is the best that I can do. The night time disturbances began to seriously affect my ability to work and cope because I was sleep deprived.

One of the hardest things about all of this for me has been the isolation from my family. I've made new friends who I can speak about the situation with. I was never able to get any support from my family. I come from a strongly Catholic Family in Wisconsin. When I confided with one of my sisters about what was going on at the ranch, it came back to me that my family wanted me to come home to Wisconsin and spend some time in a state mental hospital. It got so bad that some days I would book off work without telling John and go to my boss's house and sleep during the day. My boss knew what was going on. I started to get anxiety attacks. These are not pleasant.

You're just sort of gripped by an unseen negative force that collapses your world into a moment of complete and total panic. Everything that was going on at the ranch was wearing me down. It was like something was working on me, trying to reduce all of my defenses as a human being, and the sleep deprivation was a big part of it. That's pretty much how the first fifteen years went for me at the ranch.

I don't have the recall that John has. My memory doesn't have the interactions with the grays. I only have the effects upon my body and my mind. That's not true for July 31st, 2011. That remains one of the most fascinating days of my life. I had been told by John that some people were coming out to the ranch, but I wasn't given a whole lot of detail.

You have to understand, I really stayed out of what was going on at the ranch, and this includes the investigations, the fascination, the whole celebrity of the ranch was something I kept myself completely separated from. The ranch was just a toxic place for me.

On the day that Brandy and her two Sirians came, I was a little bit late. I was at the gym and I'd forgotten about the appointment. John called me on my cell phone and told me to get home as quickly as I could. I packed up my things and went home from the gym. When I got into the house, Brandy was at the table and there was something going on there that to this day I have difficulty describing. It was a ball of light that she had somehow created and while we were sitting in the kitchen different people began to appear in the room. I mean one moment somebody would not be there and the next moment they were there. It was as mysterious as what had been happening for the last fifteen years with the negative extraterrestrials, but this experience had a much more positive feel to it. I missed the part where Brandy released the teenage boy who committed suicide in the house. John told me that the walls heated up so much he thought the house was going to catch fire. I was given a piece of crystal to hold. Everybody was holding crystal. We went around the whole house and did prayers with Brandy, and we petitioned the negative forces to leave the house. All of this was pretty uneventful. It didn't get really crazy until we went outside.

Outside, Brandy and her two Sirians stood close together, and I was told to keep holding onto my crystal, so I did. John was beside me. Brandy and the two Sirians were saying prayers, at least I assume they were prayers. They were speaking in an incantational way. Brandy brought out a sword, and she held it up to the sky and kept praying. All of a sudden, a bunch of clouds rolled in. It was not unnatural. I had been living on that ranch for a decade-and-a-half, and I had never seen anything like it. I felt like I was in the movie *Bewitched*. Clouds rolled in all around us over the ranch, and it got very dark very quickly. Then the clouds opened up and I saw a spaceship come from behind them. I looked at John, and I said, Are you seeing what I'm seeing?

He said, Yes, it's a ship.

People were driving by and stopping. Neighbors were coming out of their houses. This event was not just seen by John and I and Brandy and her cohorts, it was seen by many others. It was so bizarre to see my neighbors out pointing up in the air. Brandy and the Sirians had all these orbs around them, and they continued to pray. I wasn't the least bit scared. It was all very calming. I knew that it was being done to protect us. It was like a movie. It was really unbelievable. It remains the most remarkable day of my life. I felt really good because everything that had been going on the ranch had been very personal for John and I, and, like I said, there was nobody to really share it with. When this ship showed up and everybody could see it, including my neighbors, I felt vindicated somehow. I felt like everything I had been bottling up inside me could be let go because all of it was real. You have to understand, there's a part of every human being that keeps telling us we're crazy when things happen that are outside our minds ability to comprehend, process, and digest.

I had never seen a spaceship like that before. Brandy said that this was our ship, meaning John and I, and that it was going to protect us. The clouds became dark and the wind picked up and suddenly we were in some kind of a storm. I could see electricity in the sky. I don't mean to keep repeating myself, but it was really amazing. A bolt of purple lightning came out of the dark clouds and struck the ground just a few feet away from Brandy. I guess it traveled under the ground and came up through her shoes, because the soles of her shoes were blown off. She didn't show any signs of distress, so I wasn't worried about her at the time.

I tried to see her a week later at a shop she ran near Phoenix. She sold crystals and other stuff and did readings for people. It was really odd, though, because after what had happened at the ranch the week before, she acted like she didn't recognize me. I didn't realize then what was going on with her. I didn't understand the profound effect the lightning strike had upon her. She had no memory of me. She had no memory of the visit to the ranch. She was a different person. It took Brandy years to get her memory back. We didn't reconnect with her for a number of years after that visit to the ranch. She reached out to us as a result of hearing us, or rather my husband, on a late night radio program, talking about the phenomenon at the ranch. It was then that we learned that she underwent a number of operations as a result of the lightning strike, and that a chunk of her memory had been erased.

The only thing she said to me that day I visited her at her shop was that I needed to contact my mother. My mother missed me, and that she wanted to hear from me. She said that to me without even realizing who I was, without knowing that I was the person at the ranch a week earlier.

I called my mother, and, in fact, it was true, she needed to hear from me. When we finally did connect with Brandy years later, she was a completely different person. When she came out to the ranch on July 31st 2011, she was a very meticulous and precise person. She was completely in control of everything that was going on. She was like a general in an army. There wasn't much levity or comedy in her personality. When we reconnected she was much lighter and easygoing, and she joked around all the time. The lightning strike completely changed her personality.

The number of people who were outside the house on that day, July 31st, 2011, was more than the number of people who had come with Brandy in the car. When the incident was over, people literally just disappeared. I didn't know at the time that these were extraterrestrials. I can tell you that they looked exactly like us. They looked like human beings.

There was a little bit of an edge to them. They look to be super healthy and every aspect of their physical being was what I would call perfect, their hair, their skin, their teeth, everything. But the moment Brandy was done they just disappeared. One moment they were there, and the next moment they were gone.

I could tell stories almost forever about the things that have happened on this ranch. The encounter with Brandy, the spaceship, and the lightning bolt is hands-down the most amazing thing that's happened, but there are a lot of close seconds. One that comes to mind took place a number of years ago. John and I were in the living room watching television. There was a rainstorm outside. We lost all power in the house and everything went dark and the television went off. Then the back hallway towards the bedrooms completely lit up. I told john that I wanted to go see what it was. He wouldn't let me. He was convinced I would be abducted. So we stayed in the living room, and we looked down the hallway, which remained lit up with this white light. And then to our astonishment, two Roman Centurions from what I assume is at least a couple thousand years ago marched right down the hallway and through the living room and out the wall. I could never make up a story like this.

It really happened. There's so many of these stories that I don't even know where to begin or end. It's just been my life for the last two-and-a-half decades. Throughout all of this, John and I have grown closer. Our bond has grown stronger. When I look back at the two and a half decades on this ranch,

I can't imagine any other life now. It has been hard, and it has been very stressful and frightening at times, but I have seen a world that very few people see. It can't be unseen. My reality is completely different than the average person's as a result of living on this ranch. It's hard not to see some sense of predestination in a situation like this. I guess I just believe at this point that I was supposed to live on this ranch with my husband, John. I don't like to get involved in the public messaging too much. I feel this is just something I was meant to experience as an individual. I certainly understand the concept of making the information public, but I just don't feel that's my mission the way my husband does.

Everything that has been told in this story is true. Robert Bigelow has made numerous offers to buy our ranch. People from the government have been here to do tests. In 2017 our story blew up and became a national story, the result of a Realtor creating a press release that got picked up by every major newspaper and news outlet in the country. I guess this gave me some kind of vindication with my family, who had not given up the idea that I was going crazy. One of the hardest things about going through something like I have gone through is that in being exposed to so much that is paranormal, it makes it more difficult for you to fit into the normal world. Even with that said, I wouldn't change what has happened.

I feel privileged to have experienced what I've experienced on this ranch and to see a perspective on life that very few people get to see. I'm not sure I want to retire and live out my years on this ranch, but it has been a very engaging time. I guess what's changed most is my understanding of God and creation, and the realization that human beings are just one of a number of races that were created by some creator. We live in different parts of this universe and other universes and sometimes they overlap each other. It's all contributed to a deeper sense of wonder I have about life, and it hasn't diminished my faith in the creator at all. It's increased it.

About the Authors

John Edmonds

John Edmonds was born in Evanston, Illinois. He moved to Arizona in the late nineteen-eighties and attended Arizona State University for social work, where he attained a master's degree. He bought Stardust Ranch on June 1st, 1996 with his wife, Joyce, and has become central to one of the most important stories to emerge in the world of exopolitics.

Bruce MacDonald

Bruce MacDonald was born in Ottawa, Ontario. He has a journalism degree from Ryerson University in Toronto, Ontario. He is the co-author of *The Light of Darkness* and *The Galactic Historian*. He works remotely as a technical writer in the fields of software and telecommunications from the Province of Limon, Costa Rica, where he lives on a small farm in the Talamanca Mountains with his wife, Rosemary.

Made in United States
Orlando, FL
21 April 2023

32302555R00124